Risk and Insurance Management Manual for Libraries

Mary Breighner, CPCU
William Payton

Jeanne M. Drewes, Managing Editor

Design by ALA Production Services.

Library of Congress Cataloging-in-Publication Data
Breighner, Mary.
  Risk and insurance management manual for libraries / Mary Breighner, William Payton ; managing editor, Jeanne M. Drewes.
    p. cm.
  An updated manual based loosely on the 1977 Insurance manual for libraries, by Gerald E. Myers.
  Includes bibliographical references.
  ISBN 0-8389-8325-1 (alk. paper)
  1. Libraries--Insurance--Handbooks, manuals, etc. 2. Libraries--Risk management. I. Payton, William, 1941- II. Drewes, Jeanne M. III. Myers, Gerald E. Insurance manual for libraries. IV. Title.
  Z683.5.B74 2005
  025.1--dc22
                                    2005011413

ISBN 0-8389-8325-1

Printed in the United States of America

05 04 03 02 01   5 4 3 2 1

Disclaimer

This manual is intended to serve as a reference guide on various aspects of risk management, including bringing to the attention of the user potential hazards or conditions related to the existence and operation of libraries. The user must make the decision on whether and how to address any hazard or condition. No liability is assumed by or through the use of any information contained in the manual.

TABLE OF CONTENTS

Preface

Risk and Insurance Management Manual for Libraries is an updated manual loosely based on the 1977 *Insurance Manual for Libraries* by Gerald E. Myers. This manual broadens the previous manuals (written solely as insurance manuals) and incorporates broader principles of risk management. The current authors are indebted to him for the previous version of the text. We also would like to express our gratitude to Norman Nelson, the original managing editor, for his patience and perseverance as we worked through this project long after early deadlines proved impossible to meet. We also are grateful to Jeanne Drewes for her guidance and contributions to the text, especially those sections relating directly to library valuations. Finally, the authors wish to thank Gerry Alonso, Barbara Carlson, Robert Fisher, Michael Frisz, Deborah Heiden, Thomas Lauer, Sandra Minor, Tim Pope, and Royce Thomas for their assistance in reviewing text and providing helpful suggestions relating to the loss prevention engineering, insurance, and claims sections of this manual. Thanks also go to Leslie Behm, Michigan State University Libraries, for her assistance in compiling the index.

Editor's Note

The creation of this updated manual was initiated in the mid-1990s by the American Library Association, the Library Administration and Management Association, and the Library Organization and Management Section's Risk Management and Insurance Committee, chaired at the time by Norman Nelson. Through the dedication and efforts of the authors, the managing editors, and LAMA Executive Director Lorraine Olley over a period of several years, this manual was eventually written and published.

It takes dedicated and knowledgeable experts committing countless hours to produce a publication such as this. It also takes the support and dedication of staff at ALA to see the manuscript through to publication. The purpose of this manual continues the tradition of the original concept envisioned in the early 1970s of a practical how-to insurance manual that provides answers to questions about insurance and the administration of a library's insurance program. Much has changed since that time in the insurance industry. If anything, the need for such a publication is even greater. This manual provides a twenty-first-century reference for public, academic, and special libraries concerning issues of risk and insurance management.

Jeanne Drewes, Managing Editor

Introduction

The Risk and Insurance Management Manual for Libraries represents a substantial rewriting, reorganization, and expansion of the *Insurance Manual for Libraries,* which was originally published by the American Library Association (ALA) in 1977. The name change is more than just semantics. While risk management and insurance are closely related, and even considered synonymous in some organizations, insurance alone is not risk management. Risk management is far broader. While it does encompass insurance, risk management also deals with the concepts of avoiding, preventing, and minimizing loss. In addition, risk management addresses methods other than insurance for transferring the financial consequences of losses that do occur. Risk and insurance management apply to all libraries, from the smallest to the largest.

The concept of a "manual" has been retained. The intention is to provide a ready reference guide, rather than a detailed text, to virtually all aspects of risk management. These include liability and property insurance lines of coverage—subjects on which a librarian, library manager, administrator, or supervisor may seek guidance. Much of the information provided, including the terms used, is generic in nature. That is, it should be applicable to most public, academic, and special libraries, both large and small, throughout the United States and Canada. Appendix A provides a list of resources for further information related to risk and insurance management for libraries.

Objectives

The manual's specific objectives are:

1. To inform trustees, directors, librarians, and other library personnel of the essential elements and concepts of an appropriate risk and insurance management program for libraries.
2. To assist those responsible for designing, implementing, and administering a library risk management program, including all members of the risk management team. Participants should include trustees, directors, and librarians, and may include underwriters, consultants, agents, and brokers.
3. To provide a guide for library personnel so an effective risk and insurance management program can be developed.

Discussion of group insurance for employees has been purposely omitted from this manual. The subject material of this manual is limited to property and casualty risk and insurance management. Employee benefits, such as medical and disability insurance, are not included because the insurance needs of employees are not unique to libraries and frequently are provided through coverage by a library's parent organization.

CHAPTER 1
A Risk Management Philosophy for Libraries

Responsibility of the Library Board of Directors or Trustees

Whether the library is a part of an institution or other organization or is a separate legal entity, the ultimate authority for its operation lies with a board of directors, trustees, or other governing body. The obligations and responsibilities of this board may be defined by state statute, or the board may, to a large extent, be subject to common law rules. In any event, there is a moral and a legal obligation calling for the exercise of good business judgment in protecting the library's assets against serious loss. This requires the directors and trustees to identify all risks of loss to which the library may be exposed as a result of its operations. Having identified the risks of loss, the directors have the ultimate responsibility to deal with those risks to minimize the adverse financial consequences of losses that may result from those risks. In short, the board is responsible for the development of a risk management policy for the library.

Directors and trustees cannot abandon their obligation for identifying risks and taking steps to minimize the risk of loss to either the library or another person or entity. The board can, however, delegate the implementation of the risk management policy to others, including the librarian, business officer, controller, treasurer, or other person. In most cases, this is what is done. Even where the library is part of a municipality, university, or larger organization, the library administrator, the controller, and the librarian must be provided with standards or guidelines. These standards or guidelines should delegate authority to identify and manage risks, including purchasing insurance. A risk management policy statement should be developed by the board and disseminated throughout the library to those responsible for carrying out business policies of the board.

What Is Risk Management?

Risk management has a variety of definitions:

- "Risk management is the identification, measurement and treatment of property, liability and personnel pure-risk exposures" (Williams and Heins 1985, 16).
- Risk management "is concerned with the systematic organized effort to eliminate or reduce harm to persons and the threat of losses to public organizations" (Reed and Swain 1990, 261).
- "Risk management can be defined as a systematic process for the identification and evaluation of pure loss exposures faced by an organization or individual, and for the selection and administration of the most appropriate techniques for treating such exposures" (Rejda 1992, 47).
- "Risk management is a broad-based, systematic approach to preventing accidental losses, reducing the cost of losses that occur, and finding the most efficient way to pay for whatever losses remain" (Trupin and Flitner 1998, 2).
- "Risk management is a discipline for dealing with the possibility that some future event will cause harm. It provides strategies, techniques and an approach to recognizing and confronting any threat faced by an organization in fulfilling its mission" (Risk Management Resource Center 2002).

No matter which definition the library prefers, risk management is a systematic process of identifying, analyzing, and quantifying the risks of human, physical, and financial loss to preserve the assets of the library by selecting the most appropriate method of managing the risks through avoidance, elimination, prevention, reduction, knowing assumption, or transfer of the risk of loss to others, or by purchase of insurance.

Risk Management and Insurance Management

Risk management is a broader concept than insurance management. It places greater emphasis on identification, analysis, prevention, and control of risks. Insurance is only one tool in the risk management process. Risk management recognizes that some risks can be avoided; that other risks can be reduced or eliminated; that still additional risks can be transferred to others; that some risks are insurable, some not; and that some risks involve types of losses that should be insured against by the purchase of commercial insurance, while others are losses that can be assumed or self-insured. Issues of primary importance in risk management are loss prevention and loss control, insurance, and communication. When fully implemented, risk management decisions have a greater impact on library operations than insurance alone and can add value to the library by helping avoid or minimize major financial losses and by making the library a safer place to learn and work. These principles are readily adaptable to libraries—large, small, public, private, or special.

The Risk Management Process

The risk management process involves several steps—all designed to help reduce uncertainty concerning the occurrence of a loss. The process consists of six steps: risk indentification, risk quantification and evaluaton, risk avoidance, loss prevention and control, risk financing, and re-evaluation.

Risk Identification

The first step in the risk management process is to determine the risks of loss to which the library is subject. This will involve an analysis of the operations of the library and identification of risks inherent in those operations. In this step, the library will identify those assets or operations that, if damaged or destroyed, would cause difficulty to ongoing operations. These include the physical assets of the library, such as the building and its collections; the human assets, including all employees and volunteers, particularly those who are specially trained in skills critical to the library's functions; financial assets that might be subject to theft; and the risks present in the library's operations, such as trip-and-fall hazards. Simply put, in this step the library is looking to determine who could be at risk as a result of the library's operations and what could be damaged, destroyed, or lost as a result of the library's operations. Chapter 2 discusses this step of the risk management process in more detail.

Risk Quantification and Evaluation

The next step in the process is to quantify the risks identified in step one. This involves an evaluation of the potential size of losses that may occur from the different risks identified and the likelihood that such losses will occur. In other words, the library will evaluate the probable frequency and severity of losses from various risks. For example, what is the likelihood of having property damaged or lost from any number of causes, such as fire, flood, or wind? And what is the estimated size of the damage that might ensue? For what operations, actions, and inactions might the library be held liable under law if such operations, actions, or inactions result in bodily injury or property damage to someone else or someone else's property? Chapter 3 discusses this step of the risk management process in more detail.

Arguably, the first two steps in the risk management process are the most critical. The more accurate these assessments are, the more effective the program designed to manage the risks can be.

Once potential risks of loss have been identified and quantified, the library needs to evaluate and select the most effective method to handle these risks. In evaluating the options, the library must balance the desire to reduce risk and prevent losses with an understanding that risks are an inherent part of any library operation. Therefore, while some risks can be eliminated without a disruption to operations, many cannot. These risks must be dealt with in a way that decreases the likelihood a loss may occur and that limits any potential financial loss to the library, yet allows the library to continue its mission of service to its constituents.

Risk Avoidance

Avoidance can be the most effective risk management strategy but for many risks inherent in the library's operations, it may not be practical or even possible in the context of the library's mission of service to its community. Yet, some risks can be avoided without causing disruption to library operations. It is advisable to eliminate risks wherever possible and feasible. For example, the library could dispose of a truck used to transport books and instead hire a public trucker for this purpose.

Loss Prevention and Control

Many risks of loss either can be eliminated or reduced significantly by loss prevention activities. Some examples include training drivers to operate more safely in order to reduce the likelihood of auto accidents; training workers in proper lifting techniques to limit the potential for injuries; and installing smoke detectors, fire alarms, and automatic sprinkler systems to prevent or limit smoke and fire damage. These are actions the library can take to reduce the likelihood of loss or minimize the losses that do occur for those risks the library accepts as part of doing business. Chapter 4 discusses this step of the risk management process in more detail.

Risk Financing

Ultimately, many risks will remain both part of the library's operations and its financial responsibility. Therefore, risk financing is a major component of the risk management process. Risk financing is the process of selecting the most cost-effective means of ensuring funds will be available after a loss to allow the library to rebuild and restore damaged or destroyed property and to continue its mission of service to its constituents. While the library can deal with the financial obligations incumbent with some operational risks, most libraries will not be able to, or desire to, be responsible for the adverse financial consequences of large losses. Risk financing involves three options: non-insurance transfer, self-insurance, and the purchase of commercial insurance.

Transferring the Risk to Others

Whenever possible, risks should be transferred from the library to others with whom it does business via a non-insurance transfer, such as "hold harmless" or indemnity clauses in contracts with third parties. An indemnity clause or hold harmless agreement written into a contract or lease agreement will provide that a third party contracting with the library will accept financial responsibility for losses caused by that third party's negligent operations on behalf of the library. Chapter 5 examines this concept in more detail.

Self-insurance

Self-insurance is defined as ". . . the conscious retention of risk, the level of which has been limited within the financial capacity of the firm, emanating from a distribution of exposures that permit reasonable predictions as to future loss probabilities" (Goshay 1964, 21). "Self-insurance" is not the same as "no insurance" in that self-insurance involves a specific decision to absorb the financial consequences of a particular loss or type of loss, after the risk of loss has been identified and quantified. Chapter 5 discusses this concept in more detail.

Purchase Insurance

As a general guideline, commercial insurance should be purchased when the probability or likelihood of loss is low but the potential severity of any loss that may occur is high. Two other types of risks also are reasons for the purchase of commercial insurance:

- those for which the law requires insurance (such as bonds on specified library employees, workers' compensation); and
- those in which the insurer may have expertise and provide valuable services that justify the purchase of insurance, even though the library has the financial capacity to absorb the losses that might be expected (such as boiler and machinery insurance).

Generally, libraries should at least consider purchasing the following types of insurance: workers' compensation; property, boiler and machinery; general and excess liability; automobile liability; directors' and officers' liability; and fiduciary liability. Chapter 6 contains a more extensive discussion of commercial insurance.

Re-evaluation

Finally, the library should re-evaluate the risk management process on a periodic basis. This is especially important if the library has opened new facilities, launched new programs, or executed non-insurance transfers.

A Risk Management Policy Statement

Risk management is an attitude that must be adopted by everyone in the library. That attitude, when adopted by all staff, leads to a safer environment for staff as well as for the library's customers. In addition, adopting a strong commitment to risk management will ensure the library's physical assets are well protected and the likelihood of loss is decreased. Because the board has the primary responsibility for establishing the risk management philosophy, it also has primary responsibility for developing and promulgating a risk management policy statement for the library's staff that lays the foundation for the risk management attitude. But simply developing a policy is not enough. It is the board's responsibility to see that its risk management policy is effectively communicated throughout the library.

The library's risk management policy statement, first and foremost, should set forth the library's philosophy regarding risk management. It should state unequivocally the library's commitment to risk identification and examination and to proactive risk management. The policy statement should designate the individual or individuals who shall have the administrative responsibility for overseeing the policy in day-to-day operations. It should delegate risk and insurance management responsibility and authority to the librarian or other person. The policy statement may provide the parameters of the authority, as well as delineate what areas will remain within the sole jurisdiction of the board. The risk management policy statement may assign responsibility for determining the form of coverage, policy terms and conditions, the amount of coverage or limits of liability, or the amount of any deductible or self-insured retention. It may designate the types of services to be used (consultants, agents, or brokers), and it may prescribe requirements relating to bidding of insurance coverage. A sample risk and insurance management policy statement is contained in appendix B.

The Librarian's Responsibility

The library and its risk and insurance management needs are unique in several ways. The library's most valuable assets are its collections. They have special valuation issues, and their services cannot be readily provided by the use of substitute facilities. In most cases, the librarian is the person who should be relied upon for much of the information essential to establishing a risk management and insurance program.

If the library is a part of an institution that employs a professional risk manager (or other officer responsible for administering risk management), the librarian should be involved in various stages of the risk management process and work with the risk manager to identify and quantify fully the risks of loss to which the library is exposed. Only after fully knowing and assessing the risks can the library develop an adequate insurance program to properly protect itself in the event of loss. Once insurance coverage has been placed, the librarian should thoroughly understand the lines of coverage that apply to the library operations and its building and contents, as well as the amount of deductibles the library may be called upon to absorb. The librarian also should understand the extent of recovery that can be expected in the event of a loss in relation to the cost of repairing the damage—in other words, how much strain, if any, may be placed upon the library's budget in the event of a probable loss.

Within the concept of risk management, there should be a well-established policy statement from the governing body or library chief executive under which the risk management principles can be applied. This policy should take into consideration the financial condition of the library, its access to additional funds for self-insured and uninsured losses, and its obligation to provide uninterrupted service to its constituents.

Whether the library is a small, public library or part of a very large institution, a risk management policy statement is desirable as a guide for the librarian. This should embody the risk-management concepts discussed throughout this manual, and it should contain parameters relating to risks to be assumed (self-insured), risks to be covered by commercial insurance, and deductibles to be accepted (refer to appendix B).

CHAPTER 2
Risk Identification

Risk identification is a search for potential sources of losses. This chapter contains a number of categories and areas to consider for insurable hazards and risks of loss, and a brief explanation of the circumstances or events that are likely to cause loss.

The library should develop a systematic approach to risk identification that might include any or all of the following:

- an operations flow chart;
- a risk analysis questionnaire;
- insurance company inspection reports;
- a review of the library's past losses;
- analysis of financial statements;
- an inspection by the library's staff;
- a review of contracts and leases the library has signed; or
- a review of local and state statutes that impose duties on the library relative to the general public, such as state statues related to workers' compensation insurance, or local statutes related to the library's obligation to provide free and clear access to its premises.

The more of these methods the library utilizes, the more thorough the identification of potential risks of loss will be. Using all the tools available will allow the library to develop the most complete risk identification. It is important to note this step can be ongoing and continuous. The library may use one or more of the tools to get started and add to the risk identification process over time. It also is important to keep in mind this process should be utilized any time new operations are undertaken that might entail new risks, such as introduction of new programs that increase the participation of the general public on the library's premises, or renovations to existing library facilities.

Major Areas of Risk of Loss

The library must identify risks from:
- physical damage to, or loss of, library property, including buildings, library books and other materials, equipment, or vehicles;

- liability losses arising from claims or lawsuits alleging negligence in the operation of the library;
- losses resulting from injury to library staff; and
- financial losses arising from unlawful acts.

Property Risks

In most instances, virtually all property owned by, leased to, or in the care, custody, or control of the library can be damaged, destroyed, or lost in the course of library operations due to any number of causes. The following lists include major items of property the library owns, uses, controls, or has responsibility for and whose loss or damage could result in financial loss or disruption of operations.

In the risk identification process the library will list all property for which it is responsible in each category. When identifying types of property potentially subject to loss, it is common to separate the property into two categories: real property and personal property. (The issues of appraisal and valuation of tangible property is discussed in chapter 3.)

Real Property

- Buildings. This category comprises all buildings owned or leased by the library, including buildings under construction, office facilities, book storage facilities, and garages. It also includes permanently affixed machinery, such as equipment used to maintain or service the building. Fire extinguishing equipment; appliances used for refrigeration, ventilation, cooking, and dishwashing; and certain outdoor fixtures, such as a flagpole or a sign attached to the library building, fall into this category. When categorizing leased property, the library must first determine whether the lease requires the library or the owner to be responsible for damage or destruction of the property.
- Landscaping, but not the land itself.

Personal Property

Personal property is generally considered all property that is movable and not permanently affixed to land and buildings. In the library, it includes such items as:

- Furniture and fixtures, including desks, chairs, lamps and other lighting, filing cabinets, book stacks, shelving, typewriters, computers, microform readers and printers, listening stations, and photocopiers.

- Machinery and equipment other than that permanently affixed to a building or used to maintain or service the building.
- Electronic data-processing (EDP) equipment, including computer hardware and software.
- Electronic data, including library records, indexes, and possibly the online catalog maintained on magnetic tapes and discs.
- Books and library materials, including periodicals, manuscripts, card catalogs, shelf lists, films, prints, audio and video tapes, recordings, digital facsimiles, drawings, artwork, cameras, projection machines, musical instruments, and related and similar equipment, and all other materials intended for the use of library patrons.
- Fine arts, rare books, antiques, original paintings, and other rare, unique, or irreplaceable items.
- Valuable papers and records, including records that have a value in excess of the actual tangible value of the cost of paper plus the cost of transcribing. These may include library catalogs (if the catalog is not electronic) and other library records, such as financial and accounting records.
- Consumable supplies and materials, such as office stationery, envelopes, library supplies, and janitorial supplies.
- Accounts receivable.
- Promotional displays, informational signs, and exhibits.
- Cash and negotiable instruments.
- Motor vehicles and bookmobiles.
- Property of others, including property belonging to the library's employees. This category may encompass a large variety of property, such as books on loan, office machines, microfilming equipment, copy machines, microform readers and printers, scanners, digital cameras, and other equipment. The responsibility of the library for these items should be clearly stated in the loan or lease agreement or contract related to the equipment.

Other Property Risks

Improvements and Betterments

This pertains to improvements in a leased building, such as permanent fixtures, new plumbing facilities, and the like, that have been made by the library as tenant under a current lease. In every case, the library should review the lease to determine whether the landlord has an obligation to replace the improvements and betterments in the event of loss or damage. If the landlord does not have this legal obligation, the library has two risks of loss:

- the cost of replacing the improvements if they are damaged or destroyed in order to continue to use the building; and
- the unamortized portion of the improvements and betterments or their use value for the unexpired terms of the lease, should the landlord cancel the lease as a result of the loss or damage.

Business Interruption

This includes lost revenue and continuing expenses that will be incurred by the library in the event of a loss that causes the library to interrupt its operations or to discontinue some or all of its services.

Extra Expense

This includes funds in excess of normal operating costs necessary to continue operations in the event that library facilities are damaged or destroyed.

An indirect loss can result from serious damage to library property in the form of extra or additional expense if the library desires to continue its services at temporary locations. The library should determine in advance whether it will need an extra fund to continue operating at temporary locations in the event of a catastrophe. If so, the library should determine the amount of extra or unusual expenses that might be necessary to continue operation, and for what period of time.

Property Perils

Property can be lost, damaged, or destroyed by virtually any cause. However, many causes of loss occur in the ordinary course of business and are not risks with which risk management is generally concerned. Risk management generally focuses on types of losses that can be prevented or minimized and those that can be financed, either by the library itself or by a third party (either a contracting party or a commercial insurer) for the benefit of the library. From a risk management perspective, the following is a list of common perils to which the library property may be subject:

- fire and lightning;
- riot, explosion, vehicle damage, smoke, hail, aircraft damage, and windstorm (including hurricanes and tornados);
- vandalism and malicious mischief;
- sprinkler leakage;
- water damage from defective plumbing, heating, or air-conditioning systems;
- collapse of buildings or structures;
- glass breakage;
- burglary, theft, robbery;
- boiler and machinery;
- property in transit;
- earthquake;
- flood, backed-up sewers, surface waters; and
- terrorism.

Sources of Liability Risks

In addition to loss involving library-owned property, the library may suffer financial loss related to injuries to people or damage to non-owned or leased property that occurs as a result of the library's operations and for which the library is responsible, either due to the negligence of library employees or agents in conducting library business, or due to statutory or regulatory imposition of responsibility. Some of the most common circumstances are listed below.

Premises

This includes building, grounds, and leased property. Liability of the library may result from negligent maintenance of the premises that results in an injury to a third party. For example, poorly lit steps, water on the floor, cracks on sidewalks, dimly lit parking facilities, incomplete snow removal, and tripping hazards may lead to liability as all could result in an injury to a third party.

Operations or Activities

This includes the actions of board members, officers, employees, agents, and volunteers. Many libraries have moved beyond reading and lending books as their only activities. Cafés, exercise and dance classes, arts and crafts programs, stage and musical performances, and even after-school care are all part of the offerings at some libraries. While these activities can enhance the value of the library experience, they also create additional exposures. Coffee served in the café may burn someone, negligent dance instruction can lead to an injured participant, and negligent supervision in arts and crafts programs can lead to injury.

Contracts or Leases

These are arrangements in which the library has agreed to indemnify or hold harmless the other party for liability for injuries arising out of the contract. (In the case of new construction, the library may be the beneficiary of such a clause wherein the contractor agrees to hold harmless the library. Chapter 7 discusses this concept in greater detail.)

Autos, Trucks, Mobile Equipment, Bookmobiles

This includes vehicles owned, leased, or hired by the library, as well as vehicles owned by others that are being driven on library business.

Intentional Torts

Torts are civil wrongs. In the course of library business any number of intentional torts may subject the library to liability. The library should consider in its risk identification process risk of loss due to libel, slander, invasion of privacy, assault, battery, false arrest, or trespass.

Directors' or Trustees' and Officers' Liability

This is another area of liability risk to which directors or trustees and officers may be subject. In the case of a nonprofit corporation or a public (governmental or quasi-governmental) body, a similar action might be brought by a member or by a citizen whom the corporation or public body is organized to serve. For example, budget constraints might lead to a reduction in communities served by bookmobiles, leading a community to file an action against the library's board.

Employment Practices Liability

This is a growing area of litigation. Library boards may have to face suits by employees who claim there has been a violation of their civil rights in hiring, promotion, or wrongful discharge based on race, sex, religion, national origin, or other characteristics.

Fiduciary Liability

This is the risk of the library to responsibly and ethically handle funds entrusted to it.

Employee Benefits Liability

This category is a relatively new exposure arising from the administration of a benefit policy for an entity's employees. An example of this would be neglecting to properly inform an employee of—or failing to register an employee for—benefits, causing the employee to suffer financial loss in the future.

LIABILITY RISKS

Bodily Injury (BI)

This category of risk includes sickness, disease, death, or mental injury allegedly suffered by library patrons or members of the general public as a result of negligence by library staff or any other person for whom the library is responsible.

Property Damage (PD)

These risks relate to physical injury to, or destruction of, tangible property, including loss of use thereof, incurred as a result of a claim of negligence in library operations; loss of use of tangible property.

Personal Injury (PI)

This risk involves libel, slander, defamation, or violation of privacy rights; false arrest, detention or imprisonment, or malicious prosecution; discrimination; or deprivation, violation, or infringement of rights.

OTHER RISKS

Injury to Employees

The risks to be considered here are injuries suffered by employees in the course of their employment. Exposure includes medical expenses, salary continuance, permanent or temporary disability, loss of limb(s), rehabilitation, and death.

Employee Dishonesty Risks

These risks relate to dishonest, fraudulent, or criminal acts committed by library employees that may result in financial loss to the library. Examples include the unlawful electronic transfer of library funds or theft from the library's petty cash fund. This risk is not limited to the library's treasurer or controller or even those in a supervisory capacity. The risk involves loss of property as well as money, and even those not directly responsible for library funds may discover ways to defraud the library.

Special Events

Sources of significant risks include:

- sale and consumption of alcohol;
- size of crowds;
- poor signage (exits, etc.);
- slippery surfaces;
- weather conditions (heat, cold, rain, wind);
- location not designated for such an event;
- event-related controversies;
- lack of adequate parking lot lighting and security;
- lack of evacuation plan; and
- slow emergency response.

CHAPTER 3
Risk Quantification
and Evaluation

In matters of risk and insurance management, knowledge is a source of added security. It is the key element in the risk and insurance management program for any library. Chapter 1 outlined the steps in the risk management process. This chapter explores further the second step, risk quantification and evaluation.

Risk quantification involves assessing, both objectively and subjectively, the potential impact of risks. If the library is to make well-informed decisions, it is critical not only to identify property and operations that present risks of loss, but also to evaluate the risks and magnitude of all the library's assets, including physical property and financial assets. Ultimately, decisions regarding risk financing, including insurance, will depend upon accurate valuation of assets, especially library collections. Not only must the library determine the value of collections, it also must identify which portions of a collection need to be restored most quickly following an interruption in service. For example, in an academic library it may be most critical to ensure the reserve collection, which contains required reading for students, is first back in service. In a public library it may be more important to ensure the children's collection is first to resume service following an interruption.

The responsibility of attaching value to the library's specific collections rests predominantly with the library staff. This can be challenging. The next section provides a broad overview of how to establish accurate values for the library's property, both real and personal. The section also includes a methodology for valuing library collections, likely the highest valued property.

Property

If the library has not determined how much it will cost to replace damaged or destroyed property, it is without a complete measure of property exposures. (The types of property, real and personal, are defined in chapter 2.) First and foremost, it is important to note that the purchase price of the library's physical assets has very little to do with the assessment of their value to the library in the event of a loss. Likewise, any recording of assets that lists them by original cost minus depreciation will not give an accurate picture of the value of library property in the event of loss or damage.

Instead, risk and insurance management relies on two other concepts to determine value. The first is actual cash value (ACV), which is defined as replacement cost at the time of loss, less depreciation. This concept also takes inflation into consideration. ACV does not necessarily result in lower values, as many believe. ACV values may actually increase if the rate of inflation exceeds the rate of depreciation. However, the impact of depreciation, which accounts for wear and tear and economic obsolescence, often results in a substantial loss of asset value. The deduction for depreciation will obligate the library to make up the difference to restore the property to its original condition, which is why most property should be valued on a replacement-cost basis.

Replacement cost is simply the cost of replacing all library-owned and leased property new at current prices. These replacement costs, replacement times, and repair times are calculated on a non-expedited basis. This method of quantifying all property identified in the first step of the risk management process will give the library the most accurate picture of the potential for loss.

Real Property Valuation

Buildings

Replacement cost, as applied to buildings, denotes the cost of replacing a complete structure and permanently affixed machinery, including equipment used to maintain or service the building. It includes the entire building: superstructure; foundations; finish work (case and cabinet work, ceiling, wall and floor coverings, painting); heating, ventilation, and air conditioning (HVAC) equipment; lighting, wiring, and electrical service equipment; fire protection devices (automatic sprinklers, valves, pumps); plumbing fixtures and piping; and other building service and utility equipment, such as fire extinguishing equipment, appliances used for refrigeration, ventilation, cooking, and certain outdoor fixtures (a flagpole or a sign attached to a building, for instance).

Also included are other permanent items, such as landscaping, pavement, fencing, underground piping and wiring, and retaining walls. All labor costs are estimated at prevailing union rates. Additionally, the replacement cost for buildings includes costs for general or unusual conditions, such as special load bearing for bookstacks, architect's and engineer's fees, permits, and other direct and indirect costs necessary for reproducing the building.

Real property values should represent complete building replacement cost, including building service equipment, such as heating, air conditioning, elevators, lighting and power wiring, and fire protection. The values assigned to library buildings also should recognize the quality of finishes, partitions, and plumbing.

Real property values should exclude excavation or other site work, and be based on the total floor area of all floors, measured from outside wall to outside wall (also referred to as the gross floor area). This measurement should be taken for all floors, including basements, finished attics, penthouses, and those mezzanines, galleries, and platforms where the individual floor area is 10 percent or more of the footprint of the building.

Structures that are not buildings, such as water towers, also should be included as real property. Values for any new buildings and additions under construction also should be included. Square footage and special construction, such as additional load bearing for bookstacks, should be documented and updated from the construction cost guides at least every five years.

When estimating a building's value, the library should consult a construction cost guide, a useful reference in determining a value per-square foot for the building structure. This guide helps the library determine value that reflects the building's construction, uniqueness of design and geographic area, and takes into consideration the end-use of the building and associated costs, such as construction needed to increase the floor-load capacity.

The Bowker Annual of Library and Book Trade Information provides many different reports. Among them is a table of "New Public Library Buildings," listed by state and by community within each state. This table can be a useful reference to help the library estimate average construction costs for library buildings within the geographical area. Note that construction costs vary greatly depending on the location and the type of library. For example, in 2001, a new branch library in the Boston area cost $315 per square foot, while a new main library in Byfield, Massachusetts, cost $134 per square foot. A new branch library in Fairfax County, Virginia, cost $229 per square foot; a new branch library in Virginia Beach, Virginia, cost $84 per square foot.

Appraisals

One of the best ways to obtain accurate property and replacement values is to have an appraisal firm conduct an onsite field appraisal. Using blueprints or actual field measurements, the appraiser will determine quantities and sizes of building components and materials. When blueprints are not available and components are situated too high to be measured, appraisers will estimate sizes by comparing them to known component sizes (bricks, masonry units, wood or steel members, ladder rungs, and so on). These techniques have produced reliable, accurate estimates.

The appraiser then discerns the replacement value of buildings and other structures by applying unit costs of the individual construction materials in place to the quantities established by the field measurements and blueprints. Costs are adjusted by region to account for local labor and material cost variances. Appraisers do not factor in costs to conform to building codes, ordinances, or other legal restrictions; cost of demolition in connection with reconstruction; or the removal of destroyed property.

Organizations such as the American Society of Appraisers (real, personal, and business valuation properties) located in Herndon, Virginia, the Appraisal Institute (real property) located in Chicago, and the National Association of Independent Fee Appraisers (real property) located in St. Louis can be very helpful in locating a reliable appraisal firm. (See appendix A for additional information.)

Improvements and Betterments in Leased Buildings

The valuation should be determined in the same manner as for buildings. If the landlord has the obligation of replacement, but also has the option of lease cancellation in the event of a loss, the measure of risk for the library usually will be the unamortized leasehold value; that is, that proportion of the original cost to the library for the improvements as represented by the unexpired portion of the lease.

Personal Property Valuation

The owned contents of the library building (personal property) can generally be divided into four categories for valuation: furniture, including book stacks and specialized storage, such as microforms and map storage; business operations information; computers, software, and computer files, which usually includes the online catalog; and physical collections, which include books, maps, audio-visual materials, journals, manuscripts, and rare materials. Physical collections, because they tend to include both older and new materials, often are most difficult to value. Within collections, the distinction between general circulating collections and special or rare materials also should be noted for valuation purposes.

The library staff is often better prepared than a general appraiser to take responsibility for placing a value on library collections. In the case of vehicles, furniture, exhibits, consumables, office equipment, copiers, readers and printers, and computers, the replacement value can be determined through an inventory. Replacement costs for personal property include the cost of replacing all facility contents with the same or similar new items as well as fees for shipping and installation, equipment and material, testing and commissioning, and warranty and service. Replacement time includes engineering and design, date of order to date of shipment, normal transportation time, installation time, and testing and commissioning periods, all to be calculated at the time of loss. A good inventory control practice is essential for verifying materials destroyed in a loss. It is vital to update the inventory as equipment is replaced or upgraded in order to provide accurate records for valuation.

As with books, computers and most software are considered standard library contents. An up-to-date inventory of computer hardware and software also is important to an effective valuation because libraries now depend on computers to access titles in electronic formats.

All equipment lease agreements, such as those for copiers or computers, should clearly state the responsible party in the event of loss. If the library is the responsible party, it must update the valuation of leased equipment. On-loan materials also fall under this category, and interlibrary loan material agreements should clearly state the responsible party in the event of loss.

A detailed inventory that includes valuations for all property is essential both for arriving at an accurate risk assessment and for establishing or proving a loss. The more detailed the description of each item, the easier it is to establish value at the time of loss. However, it is not necessary to list minor items. Instead, these usually can be grouped together when the total amount is not large.

Suggested methods of establishing the base value are as follows:

- If the original cost and year of purchase are available, values can be trended from cost tables to current prices, providing the original purchase information is not older than the maximum useful life of the trends. In the case of a relatively new library, original purchase records may be readily available.

- The librarian or an assistant can make an inventory, and price each item or each group of items from current catalogs. Installation costs for communications equipment that is not a part of the building value and for electronic data processing (EDP) equipment should be included.

Values for buildings and contents alike should be brought up to date annually by the use of the latest cost indices. For updating replacement cost values, the library may refer to insurance carriers or Marshall and Swift/Boeckh (see appendix A).

Appraisals

An appraiser hired to do a real property valuation also can be retained to inspect and individually list contents of furniture and business operations information. Typically, the appraiser lists enough information about the equipment so its replacement cost may be properly researched upon return to his or her office. Relatively low-value, high-quantity items, such as furniture, fixtures, small machinery and equipment, and personal computers, are grouped and totaled. In the office, equipment replacement prices are researched and totaled. To the new price of the equipment, a value is added to cover freight, taxes, foundation, and installation. Also included, if necessary, is value to cover unusual conditions that would be encountered in association with acquiring and installing equipment, such as obtaining licenses, certification, and so on. They are also included to develop the full replacement value.

Appraisals conducted for general insurance purposes, including buildings and contents, typically will value items such as fine arts, rare books, historical artifacts, archival documents, paintings, and sculptures at their decorative, functional value purpose only—not at replacement cost. A specialized appraisal is needed to determine replacement costs for these library properties.

Books and Library Materials

For general library collections and rare materials, usually the librarian can best assess replacement value using standard library tools unfamiliar to insurance appraisers. General collections can be valued by setting an average value within a subject area. For special or rare collections, individual pieces above a certain amount should be scheduled with values set by title, or piece or collection.

General Collections

The majority of libraries today use some sort of online catalog for documenting collections, providing circulation services and access for the public. In most cases, these online systems can provide a wealth of information about the collection, which can be used by librarians for valuation. Because material value varies greatly by subject and because replacement value is far different from purchase price after a certain age, even circulating collections can be undervalued. Most libraries keep statistics on the total number of pieces in a collection for annual reports and other statistical reporting. However, more granularity is necessary to assure accurate valuation if collections cover more than one subject area or if the collection spans a long period of copyright dates.

Book dealers and library book jobbers can provide a wealth of information about the current price of materials by subject. That information, coupled with reports acquired through the online catalog, can provide a useful and highly accurate valuation. Because most losses are partial, the grouping of collections by location, in addition to subject, is important to consider in the valuation. In the case of a partial loss to the most expensive portion of the collection, the importance of accurate valuation by location and subject is obvious.

Determining the most likely fire scenario will help the library determine the best method for grouping materials. For example, separating the collection by building wing is recommended in a case where the library is one multistory building yet houses two separate heating and cooling units. This separation is suggested because the most likely fire scenario would result in partial loss on multiple floors in only one wing, rather than in both wings of the building.

Determining the value of library collections is a formidable task. Many municipalities have large library buildings with extensive general collections, while others also maintain additional collections in neighborhood libraries and bookmobiles. The total number of items involved is so great that individual pricing is not practical. The solution is to develop an average value for each category within each location. Generally, the better categorized the collection, the more accurate the values.

Here are some tips to help the library reach an accurate determination of collection values:

- Divide monograph titles from serial titles to estimate values by titles. Using the online catalog, determine the number of monograph titles per call number division, and then do the same for serial titles.
- Compile a physical volume count for serials in addition to the title count. Taking an average number of physical volumes per title and by subject is a good method for determining a per-volume replacement value for serial titles.
- Sort the collection by format and location using the online catalog. This allows the library to determine values for such formats as audiotapes and DVDs separately from book formats.
- Include the cost of processing in the replacement cost estimate. The cost of ordering, processing, and shelving a library volume varies widely across the country because of different salary scales for staff.

Most libraries have a fairly accurate count of the number of volumes in their collection, but the number of volumes broken down into format (periodical, monograph, or nonprint) within each subject is sometimes unknown. Online catalogs or automated card catalogs of library holdings often provide the number of held titles, but they generally do not give a volume count. If a collection has bar codes used for discharging and charging materials to patrons, then a more accurate number of physical volumes can be determined. In the past, volume and title counts were difficult to determine. Today's library management systems allow this task to be accomplished more efficiently.

The breakdown of volumes by subject is important to determine the value of a general collection. Many book jobbers can provide average cost by subject and, in some cases, such values are provided free on Web sites. *The Bowker Annual of Library and Book Trade Information* and *Blackwell Book Services—US Approval Coverage and Cost Study* are useful sources of information on current purchase prices for most library materials. These reference guides, found in most libraries, make it relatively easy to determine price by subject and format, and can help the library establish a replacement value for most items. To arrive at an accurate estimate of value, however, the source figure must be used in conjunction with the number of volumes by subject and format in each library location.

Once a complete valuation is made for a collection, new volumes can be added each year. However, the library should periodically re-value the collection to estimate accurately the replacement costs of materials using current pricing. It is suggested a valuation be completed every five years. In addition, the library should conduct an annual review to determine the total number of items in each category of books and library materials, and to apply appropriate average prices to each. Normally, this entails an adjustment of the previous year's inventory by additions and deletions.

Following are the values of various contents found in different libraries. These are not absolute amounts, but they give the library an indication of the figures with which it will be working in the valuation.

Periodicals

Below are some 2000 values for periodical subscriptions according to *Bowker.* Note the large differences in prices by subject:

- average periodical price: $241.54
- children's periodicals: $25.14
- general interest periodicals: $44.48
- history: $63.12
- home economics: $115.57
- physical education and recreation: $51.87

Books

Hardcover book values for 2000 are nearly as varied:

- average hardcover book price: $60.84
- arts: $53
- general: $50.31
- biography: $45.31
- juvenile: $22.71
- fiction: $25.75
- sports, recreation: $40.64
- travel: $40.27
- other formats:

  - video cassettes: $77.85
  - audio cassettes: $8.20
  - compact discs: $12.65
  - CD-ROM titles (values vary significantly by subject): 1999 average: $20.07

Note that all sources give average prices for various categories of materials. When using these figures as a basis for valuation, the library should keep these points in mind:

- The list prices of the newly published materials are average retail prices. Adjustments must be made for a variety of factors, including geographic price variations, shipping and handling charges, and any discounts available to the library.
- The library's costs of processing and reshelving are not included in these prices.
- *Bowker* and *Blackwell* data are only two guides that may be useful. Librarians in special libraries, such as law, medicine, and engineering, may get assistance directly from publishers in those fields.
- Over a period of several years, librarians who wish to analyze their own purchases may be able to rely on their own average costs or make adjustment in *Bowker* or other reference source costs based on their purchases.
- Average discounts being realized by the library in its purchases should be included in the calculation.
- The library should reduce the total value by an amount representing the estimated value of books and library materials out on loan.

Many library book companies now maintain Web sites with useful breakdowns of cost by subject. Often, these breakdowns are much more detailed than what was once available in *Bowker.* One such example is YBP Library Services. Their Web site, available without subscription at www.ybp.com/ybp/DomIndex. html?book_price_update.html&1, provides a detailed breakdown by Library of Congress or Dewey classification. Pairing this with the number of volumes in each call number category using a report or search function in the online catalog can provide a very detailed valuation. However, as noted above, before the library begins a valuation by subject, it should first divide the collection by location.

A software package to calculate the accumulated numbers of volumes and the per-unit value can provide a much more accurate replacement value. While this method works well for monograph titles, serials require a slightly different method. For monograph titles, multivolume sets are assumed to be figured into the cost breakdown by call number. For serial collections, the acquisitions module of the online catalog often can be used to determine current subscription price as well as number of titles and volume count. These three reports can provide a reasonable average price for serials within classification breakdowns similar to the method given for monograph titles. Again, dividing the values by location is useful in the event of a partial loss.

Government documents, whether international, national, or state, may come free of charge to a library if it is part of the depository system. These materials also should be valued using the subject categories for monographs and serials determined in the method above. Governments do not replace lost items, so it is the responsibility of the holding library to insure against their loss.

Maps, posters, photographs, and art collections also may be a part of the general collection. The library should include location and replacement value in the totals for the general library collections.

Other Assessment Needs

Other parts of the collection also need to be assessed, including loaned or borrowed materials, rare books, fine arts, valuable papers, government documents, and computer hardware and software.

Borrowed Materials

Every library borrows materials through interlibrary loan, and some items might be in the library at the time of a disaster. The responsibility for loaned or borrowed items should be clearly stated in the loan agreement. If the borrowing library is responsible for these materials, they should be included in that library's risk quantification.

Special Collections

The special collections of local and rare materials should be separately inventoried and valued by item for materials valued over a set amount. There should be yearly updating of the collection valuation based on donated materials and auction prices for any similar rare books held in the collection. Property should always be identified with a specific or stated value for each item (or group of similar items).

Rare Books, Fine Arts, and Valuable Papers

By their nature, these items present unique problems when trying to establish values. For example, precisely what constitutes a rare document? Generally, such items have intrinsic value greater than the purchase price. The category might include original manuscripts, signed works, original maps, scientific documents, and documents that are no longer in print. A typical value for itemizing is in excess of $1,000 per title, though libraries with large collections may choose to set that figure higher. Yearly updating of values for rare materials is recommended to assure appropriate valuation.

Rare documents, once defined, should be inventoried to determine the size and nature of the items in the collection. One way to place a value on these items is to have them appraised, a costly process that is not often done, except for items of exceptionally high value. A professional in the field should price fine arts, original sculpture or paintings, rare books, and similar materials that have no readily determinable market or replacement value. This may be a librarian for rare books, manuscripts, and other rare or irreplaceable library materials, and a local art dealer for original paintings, sculptures, and so on.

Short of an appraisal, the librarian can establish a value for these items. For letters and manuscripts by writers, as well as original music compositions, value can be established by reviewing auction values of similar writers or composers, or by citing the paid price and allowing for inflation every year thereafter.

It is important that these types of property are identified with a specific or stated value for each item (or group of similar items). In the case of irreplaceable materials, the loss of a single item could be substantial. Establishing the general condition of these materials, with a visual record of the condition of the most valuable materials where possible, is key to establishing the values at risk for these items.

Computer Hardware and Software

As with books, computers and most software are considered standard library contents. An up-to-date inventory of computer hardware and software is important to an effective valuation because libraries now rely on computers for access to many titles produced and made available electronically.

Liability

It is easy to understand how physical damage to a library resulting from a fire or severe weather can cause a substantial loss of the library's assets. One can literally sift through the ashes or the storm debris and look at what once was. It is much more difficult to visualize the impact on assets from a liability claim. Yet the impact can be significant and, while unlikely, even surpass the value of the physical structure of the library.

However, before the library can quantify the potential costs of a liability claim, it is necessary first to understand how such a claim may arise. Generally, liability claims arise from a civil wrong committed against another party. Such a civil wrong, or injury, is known as a tort. The courts generally recognize torts as compensable wrongs.

Torts typically arise when a duty or obligation to another party is not fulfilled. For example, the library has a duty to provide a safe environment for those who use its facilities. Slippery floors, which could cause a fall, or unsafe stacking of books, which could cause injuries, are both potential torts if someone is injured due to the unsafe conditions. (It is important to note the duty or obligation cannot arise from a breach of contract, which has its own body of law.) A tort also may arise from violation of a legal right that has been imposed by law. For example, library employees have the right to expect to work in an environment free of sexual discrimination or sexual harassment. Failure to provide such an environment may be deemed tortious conduct on the part of the library if an employee feels that these rights have been violated.

It is difficult to quantify the value of a claim that has not occurred or may never occur. There is no tangible and specific asset at risk. The liability that can result from a tort can vary from the cost of a damaged vehicle or lost book to the cost of long-term care for someone seriously injured in an accident. If the incident is considered to be particularly egregious, judges and juries can award punitive damages far beyond actual economic damages.

However, it is possible to make some judgments about the cost of a liability claim should the worst happen. In today's increasingly litigious environment, there are many examples of juries sympathetic to claimants recommending exceptionally large awards seemingly out of line with the wrongdoing leading to the claim.

In an assessment of such a potential liability, the library should consider:

- The litigious nature of the community the library serves. Some states, counties, and cities have developed reputations as extremely liberal in awarding large judgments to plaintiffs. And even if the local jurisdiction has no such reputation, today almost no venue is considered immune to severe awards.
- The nature of claims and issues that have been successfully litigated against other libraries in the home state. Consider any current legal trends concerning libraries or their boards. Has the library had to cut service to surrounding communities?
- The nature of claims against business in general. Is there any civil unrest in the community that could result in actions against the library?

- The worst-case scenario. What are the one or two most catastrophic claims that could happen as a result of a tort? Imagine the worst that could happen and then increase the potential cost exponentially. For example, consider the possibility of an incident that could result in multiple deaths or long-term injuries stemming from a fire or building collapse due to the library's negligence in maintaining safe premises.

Once these issues have been considered, the library should be able to determine how to fund this worst-case scenario, generally though the purchase of insurance.

CHAPTER 4
Loss Prevention

Once the library has identified risks and estimated the potential frequency and severity of loss exposures, the next step is to select the most appropriate risk management tool or combination of tools.

The basic risk management tools include avoidance, loss prevention and control, and risk financing. As discussed in chapter 1, risk avoidance involves eliminating identified risks wherever possible and feasible. As its name implies, risk avoidance is a very effective way of controlling risk. However, in many instances, this is not practical if the library is to continue its mission of ongoing service to its constituents. Loss prevention and control, however, can be very effective and will be discussed at some length in this chapter.

Loss prevention and control are those activities designed to reduce both the frequency and severity of potential losses. They are activities that change the characteristics of risks to reduce the likelihood of loss or to reduce the severity of those losses that do occur. Loss prevention and control activities include driver education, early treatment of injuries, and use of heat detectors, automatic sprinkler systems, and burglar alarms.

Loss prevention at the library covers a broad range of risks and activities. Because of the value of the library's collection, loss prevention for the collection will be the major focus of activities in this area. As a storage place for literature, knowledge, and often priceless materials, the collection is obviously an extremely valuable asset to the library and its users. This chapter will focus on what can be done to prevent a disaster at the library and to minimize the extent of any losses that do occur.

The term "fireproof" is an anomaly when applied to a library building. Libraries' contents are combustible, and even the most fire-resistant structure will suffer heavy damage if a fire continues unchecked. Losses, no matter how well-insured, are costly, time-consuming, and frustrating, and they divert resources, both human and economic, away from the library's mission of providing service to its patrons. It is advisable, therefore, that the library utilize all resources reasonably available to prevent loss. Libraries require a superior fire protection system for three key reasons: the library is a central resource to its users, some libraries have special collections comprised of irreplaceable items and materials of great value, and the librarian has an obligation to provide safe premises and a safe working environment.

Property Loss Prevention and Control

There are a number of opportunities for the library to minimize exposures: preplanning during construction of a new facility or during a major renovation of an existing building; installing physical protection, such as automatic sprinkler protection, smoke and heat detectors, and effective vertical and horizontal cutoffs; maintaining good housekeeping; maintaining and controlling ignition sources, such as smoking, electrical systems, and hot work; and preplanning for emergency response in the event of a disaster.

Construction

If the library has plans for a new building or an addition to the existing structure, it is necessary to review the geographic building codes and standards to confirm they are consistent with current design plans. Construction requirements would have been determined as part of the exposure analysis. In coastal areas or flood zones, for example, the building construction would take into consideration the propensity for flood and surface water damage. In California and the New Madrid areas, construction would address the potential for earthquakes. In the Northeast, considerations would reflect concerns with the weight of ice and snow on roofs. The librarian should have access to the National Fire Codes and the standards and recommended practices prepared and published by the National Fire Protection Association (NFPA) (see appendix A for contact information). Specifically, NFPA Code 909, *Code for the Protection of Cultural Resources*, 2001 ed., was prepared by the Technical Committee on Cultural Resources and discusses general principles applying to library building construction, equipment and facilities, and fire protection equipment. It is worth noting the following statements from NFPA Code 909:

> This code shall prescribe minimum requirements for the protection of cultural properties and their contents from fire through a comprehensive fire protection program. (NFPA 2001, 1.2.1)

Nothing in this document shall be intended to prevent the use of systems, methods or devices of equivalent or superior quality, strength, fire resistance, effectiveness, durability and safety to those prescribed by this document. (NFPA 2001, 1.4.1)

Some insurance companies will provide assistance in reviewing construction plans and making recommendations regarding fire safety systems, which will help prevent losses. When new construction is planned, the library should make clear to architects that loss prevention, particularly related to the fire hazard, is a priority for the library. The library also should optimize the following design principles for fire protection:

- building construction and height;
- types and location of windows;
- locations and type of heating and cooling and storage facilities;
- stairway design (such as whether stairways are open or enclosed);
- use of subdivisions to prevent fire spread;
- fire control systems, including detection and suppression;
- fire department access; and
- HVAC systems that control the spread of smoke in the event of fire.

In addition, the building construction should address the means to prevent other loss exposures, such as the location of roof drains, HVAC lines, and water lines. Basement occupancies should be minimized because these often are exposed to flooding, water collection, or sewer backup. Floors should be sealed to prevent any water penetration—from sources such as sprinklers, fire hoses, water coolers, rest room facilities, and air conditioning—from passing between floors. Consideration also should be given to providing drains on each floor.

Physical Protection

If fire and burglary losses are to be minimized, prompt responses by the fire and police departments are essential. Automatic alarms are effective for this purpose. Appendix A to the NFPA Code 909, 2001 ed., provides examples of "Representative Fires in Libraries." It contains the following statement: "Damage has been directly proportional to the promptness of discovery, the transmission of an alarm . . ." (NFPA

909, 2001, 35). The value of the library's services to its constituents clearly justifies expenditure for alarms.

There is a wide variety of approved fire alarm systems. These may consist of heat- or smoke-detection units or a combination of both. To be effective, a system should cover the entire building. Local bells or sirens should be provided to warn occupants of danger, and there should be a direct connection to the fire or police department or a central station. Burglar alarms are available in an even wider variety.

Of all the risks to which the library is exposed, fire presents the greatest likelihood of severe loss. For that reason, fire protection should be the library's primary consideration. Even a small fire can spread rapidly in a library, given the concentration of combustible material. In addition, the maze-like configuration of collection stacks within most libraries can make the evacuation of occupants difficult. A fire department's first priority is always the safe evacuation of building occupants, meaning that controlling and extinguishing the actual fire is typically placed on hold until the fire department is assured all occupants are out of the structure. While saving the collection and building is vitally important, it will not be the first priority for the fire department if lives are at risk. As a result, smoke and heat detection, alarm systems, and automatic sprinklers provide the most effective and reliable fire protection for libraries and their collections.

Because of the high value of the library building and, especially, its contents, automatic sprinklers are the best form of protection in the event of a fire. It is relatively easy to freeze-dry and restore books damaged by water. It is almost impossible to restore a book that has been damaged by fire. Automatic sprinklers will control and extinguish a small fire, preventing the spread of the fire to other areas. No other form of fire protection approaches the effectiveness of automatic sprinklers. The statement above from NFPA continues: "Damage has been directly proportional to . . . the availability of automatic fire suppression . . ." (NFPA 909, 2001, 35). As a result, sprinklers are becoming a more common fixture in libraries. The Library of Congress currently uses wet-pipe sprinklers. One reason for this increasing acceptance is the fact that water from fire hoses causes more damage in larger areas than sprinklers do. Sprinklers pour water directly on the site of the fire, extinguishing it and reducing the necessity for higher volumes of water at greater pressures from fire department hoses. According to NFPA, "Records show that 70 percent of fires in sprinklered buildings have been controlled or extinguished by four sprinklers or fewer" (NFPA 909, 2001, 29).

Appendix J to NFPA 909 provides results from tests conducted by FM Global research. Those tests were conducted to answer the following questions: would fire be expected to spread in a book stack?; and if so, will automatic sprinklers keep the damage to a minimum? Two tests were made and in both cases, the answers were emphatically, "yes."

For the first fire test, standard automatic sprinklers were installed in library book stacks. In this test, one sprinkler opened in the second tier three minutes, forty-three seconds after the fire was lighted and one sprinkler opened in the first tier seven minutes, fifty-three seconds after the start. The sprinkler discharge stopped the spread of fire in the books almost immediately and gradually extinguished the fire. There was fire damage to books in 10 percent of the storage space of the stack, and this damage would be repairable for practically all the books involved. Books in an additional 27 percent of the storage space of the test segment were wet in varying degrees ranging from damp to soaked. All books involved would be repairable by drying. Heating deformed some shelf sections, although the structural members of the stack were unharmed except for paint damage.

In the second test, the same method of ignition was used to start a fire in unsprinklered stacks. Eighty-nine percent of the books were charred deeply or completely destroyed, 2.5 percent were scorched, and the remaining 8.5 percent were soaked. Approximately three-fourths of the shelving was irreparably damaged. Some of the structural elements were visibly deformed; others would not be safely reusable for live loads. These observations indicate that complete collapse of the structure was imminent when hose streams were applied.

Automatic sprinklers are generally effective only if water is available in adequate quantity at adequate pressure or if a library has its own onsite water supply. Therefore, installing automatic sprinkler protection also may require a water pump (commonly referred to as a fire pump) to provide adequate water for the sprinklers. Unless there is water available to the sprinkler system and the sprinkler control valve is open, the sprinkler system will not work. For this reason, complete loss prevention protection requires that sprinkler control valves remain open and be monitored on a regular basis. Chains and locks help keep sprinkler control valves in the wide-open position.

A sprinkler valve in the fully closed or partially closed position is described as impaired protection. In this state, sprinklers might not be as effective as with valves fully open. Typically, this impairment might occur when sprinkler valves are closed during renovation and repair work and then left closed, or when a maintenance person tests for system leaks and only partially opens the valve. These situations restrict the necessary volume of water needed to control a fire. For this reason, contractors should never be allowed unsupervised access to the sprinkler valves; instead, a member of the library staff or the facilities management or maintenance staff should operate valves at all times and keep a record of both closures and reopening of the valves. They also should ensure fire hazards are minimized during this time.

Until complete sprinkler protection can be provided, a practical combination of sprinklers and fire alarms can be designed so there are sprinklers in all high-hazard areas, especially those containing substantial combustible contents, such as workrooms or supply rooms. Heat- and smoke-detection devices with a central station connection should be provided in all other parts of the building at least until fixed protection can be provided.

The library can minimize any interruption to the use of the library by carefully planning the installating of protection, such as water supply and sprinkler risers with floor valving. This could be followed by sprinkler installations on individual floors timed to the periods of least use. Feed mains could be installed next, followed by smaller piping. Considerations should be given to prefabricating as much pipe as possible.

In addition to the NFPA code referenced above, the American Society for Industrial Security in 1997 produced "Suggested Guidelines in Museum Security," which apply to libraries as well as museums. Section 5 of the guidelines, dealing with fire protection, can be found in appendix C of this publication.

Good Housekeeping, Control of Ignition Sources

Assuming the library already has suitable construction, automatic sprinklers where needed, and an adequate water supply, good housekeeping practices and control of ignition sources are necessary steps to prevent and control property losses. The importance of good housekeeping cannot be overstated. It can minimize the causes of fire and decrease the likelihood of other property losses. Blocked doorways, halls, or exits can hinder firefighters or emergency personnel from responding promptly and properly to an emergency. This can result in a diminished ability to control and fight a fire, increased loss of library property, and possible injury to patrons and employees. Good housekeeping is a simple, yet effective, means for minimizing loss.

Enforcing no-smoking policies in all areas of the library greatly decreases the risk exposure from fire. Each lit cigarette represents a potential million-dollar fire loss. For that reason, the library should post no-smoking signs throughout the facility. The library should enforce these policies not only for employees and patrons, but also for contractors and other vendors on the library premises. This can be particularly important during construction, because contractors typically work in areas containing large amounts of combustible material but do not have working fire alarms or sprinkler protection. While most libraries have no-smoking policies, policies may fail due to lack of enforcement or lack of consequences for noncompliance.

Regular maintenance of boilers, pressure vessels, and electrical equipment—such as the systematic testing and inspection of electrical equipment and installations to ensure reliable and safe operation—not only will prolong the life of the equipment, but will also help prevent major losses. Damaged electrical wiring, unapproved computers, combustible material placed too close to electrical equipment, exposed live conductors located below baseboard heaters, and overloaded circuits, for example, all increase the likelihood of losses. To prevent these types of losses, the library should establish an electrical preventive maintenance program. Components of such a policy address such tasks as keeping electrical equipment clean, cool, and dry; keeping electrical and mechanical rooms free of combustible storage; controlling the use of portable heaters; using only qualified personnel for electrical work; and having electrical work inspected per codes.

Even if the library is fully protected by automatic sprinklers, the sprinklers will be effective only if sprinkler-control valves remain open. Sprinkler-control valves should be chained and locked in the wide-open position. To be sure automatic sprinkler systems work when needed, the library should ensure regular inspections are performed to verify valves are open. Again, this is particularly important during renovations, repairs, or construction, when maintenance personnel or contractors close valves and may not fully reopen them.

The library should include inspections of sprinkler control valves as part of regular fire safety inspections. Fire doors and fire extinguishers should be inspected monthly. Inspection records should be kept on file as evidence of good housekeeping practices.

A hot-work policy should be established and strictly enforced. Hot work is any temporary operation involving open flame or producing heat or sparks. This includes, but is not limited to, brazing, cutting, grinding, soldering, thawing pipe, and torch-applied roofing activities. A hot-work policy should require that alternative procedures be considered in lieu of hot work whenever possible. However, when hot work is necessary, it should be well-controlled by a policy that defines roles for all involved, specifies clear authority, designates hot work areas, provides fire watches, manages contractors, and conducts internal audits of how the policy is being implemented.

Appendix D provides a sample property loss prevention checklist.

Emergency Response Plan

Even with sound prevention and protection measures in place, fires and other disasters can occur. It is important to return to the risk identification analysis and consider and plan for possible emergencies and loss scenarios.

The library should develop a written emergency plan detailing areas of responsibility and those responsible for each area should work as a team. The emergency response team should hold regular meetings. Some of the essential personnel will include an emergency coordinator, someone to notify the fire department, a sprinkler-valve person, and someone to call an ambulance or police, if needed. In the event of a fire, salvage and recovery plans are required to protect the collection. Such activities can include the emergency removal of materials, covering of collection shelves, installation of dehumidifiers, and freeze-drying of wet books.

The library may build rapport with a salvage and recovery company in advance of any loss by asking the company to visit the facility to conduct an educational survey. The company could make suggestions to the library staff about what to do in the first hour after a loss—one of the most critical time periods for restoration. The firm also can be on call for emergencies.

Once the emergency plan is developed, the library should test, update, and modify it as needed. A properly orchestrated action plan can do more to protect the people and contents than almost any other action the library can take.

Protection from Weather- and Other Natural Catastrophe-Related Losses

Assuming the library already enjoys suitable construction, good housekeeping practices, automatic sprinklers where needed, and an adequate water supply, the most basic measures the library can take to prevent weather-related losses are:

- creating an emergency response team;
- routinely inspecting and maintaining the library buildings and systems;

- avoiding locating valuable collection materials in below-grade spaces and spaces that could flood; and
- properly maintaining roofs and their drains.

The emergency response team, comprised of people familiar with the library's facilities, is trained to react to emergencies resulting from specific weather conditions such as floods or windstorms. During all threatening weather events, this team would manage all loss prevention and control activities, such as:

- turning off circuit breakers and power supplies;
- ensuring sprinklers valves are open and fire pumps are operating;
- notifying the fire department, if appropriate, or other emergency response personnel (such as law enforcement, medical);
- helping library personnel safely evacuate the premises or find suitable shelter;
- helping cover vulnerable materials, such as book stacks, computers, office equipment, and catalogues, with plastic tarps; and
- helping with restoration (including freeze drying, mopping up water, and relocating wet or damaged materials).

Hurricanes and Windstorms

Additional steps the library can take to minimize damage from severe storms include:
- ensuring proper construction at the outset, and paying close attention to building maintenance;
- regularly checking perimeter roof flashing to ensure it is securely fastened;
- making sure gravel is evenly dispersed over the roof; and
- moving water-sensitive equipment away from windows or covering them with plastic tarps.

Floods

The library can minimize loss due to flooding by:
- maintaining and routinely testing sump pumps; and
- moving important records, as well as high-value equipment and supplies, to a floor above the highest floor expected to flood.

Winter Storms

The library can minimize risk from winter storms by:
- scheduling a winter inspection program and repairing significant areas of concern;

- ensuring roofs do not reach maximum snow load before they are cleared;
- always keeping roof drains and downspouts clear and flowing, even if snow cannot be removed from entire roof;
- routinely checking heating systems and water tanks to prevent freezing, which often leads to burst pipes or incapacitation of fire pumps and automatic sprinkler systems.

Appendix F applies to hurricanes, storms, and floods.

Earthquakes

Steps the library can take to minimize earthquake damage include:
- properly maintaining bracing of sprinkler and other water and gas piping; and
- installing and maintaining a seismic shut-off valve on the building's main gas line to prevent fire following an earthquake. Earthquake-actuated shut-off valves, unlike excess-flow valves, stop the flow until it is safe to restart. They often are provided directly on small, flammable gas lines. In other designs, flow in a pipe can be stopped, or other processes shut down, by a signal sent from a separate seismic sensor to a control panel or valve.

Preventive Activities

Online Catalogs

The business of the library is making information available and the key to the business is the online catalog. No amount of insurance covering that information—and few protective devices—can equal the value of a duplicate copy stored at another location. The online catalog is essential as proof of the loss sustained in a catastrophe, and it is equally useful as a guide to the librarian in replacing books and materials. For these reasons, preventing loss of the online catalog is essential. The best loss prevention method is to make regular and frequent backups of information and to store the backups in a safe place. A safe location is one other than the library building, whether that is another building remote from the library, another branch, or a different public library. (In the case of a public library, a prearranged agreement to store each other's backups may be needed.)

Computer Files

The proliferation of computer files and EDP equipment in libraries creates some special problems in protection. As the library increases its use of, and therefore its dependency on, computer equipment and magnetic tapes or disks, CD-ROMs, or DVDs for storage of information, it increases its catastrophice risk. But in most cases, information is also being stored on servers and providing that same information on a remote mirror server is the best means of protection. Duplicating the bulk of the library's records and maintaining updated duplicates at a detached location is the best loss prevention method available.

Computer Hardware and Software

As with books, computers and most software are considered standard library contents. The main computers or servers should be located in a well-isolated area without public access. The room itself should be of noncombustible construction, and the contents should exclude combustible materials, such as manuals, tape storage, or paper or plastic products. The room should be provided with central station smoke detection and some form of physical protection, such as sprinklers or fire-suppressing gas. If a computer room is particularly critical to the library's operation, both forms of protection should be provided.

Digital image files also are standard fare in most libraries, either for access to specialized collections through the Internet or on locally mounted files. In some cases, reserve collections (required reading for particular class work) are electronically accessed. While remote access to materials via the Internet is one solution used in the event of disaster, it is vitally important that locally mounted files are backed up and stored offsite. Moreover, a provision for use of other computer servers in the event of a disaster also is important for libraries to offer necessary services with little interruption. Not only is an agreement for use necessary but also testing the process to assure that files can be mounted on equipment and run at the backup location. Testing to assure compatibility is critical.

Valuable Papers and Records

These include those records that have a value in excess of the actual tangible value of the cost of paper plus the cost of transcribing. Many library records, such as financial and accounting records, may have an intangible value and be extremely costly to duplicate. Maintaining a duplicate set of these records at an off-site location, and regularly updating and backing up these documents, is a good solution to the potential loss of these records.

Rare Books and Manuscripts

The library can minimize damage to rare materials by establishing a conservation service before any loss occurs. Because the majority of repairable property damage in a fire is caused by water, immediate attention to water damage can drastically reduce the cost of restoring materials to their predisaster condition. A visual record of the condition of most valuable materials can help determine the amount of conservation treatment required. For very old materials that may already have damage or considerable wear, it is difficult to determine the actual cost of conservation for a known incident without having first established the item's predisaster condition. If this precaution is not taken, disputes could result, impeding the chances for a quick settlement.

Outside Protection and Security

Even though police patrols may provide some protection against vandalism and break-ins, their efforts may be hindered by the design of the library building and layout of library grounds. The aesthetic value of beautiful landscaping and soft lights may have to be sacrificed in favor of clear space and spotlights to discourage prowlers and unauthorized entry. Arson by means of the book return is an issue. Book returns need to be constructed in a way that precludes a fire in case someone stuffs the book return with combustibles or ignited materials.

Protection from Theft

Theft of individual books and other library materials has reached serious proportions in some libraries. Several systems of sensitizing books and library materials are now available for use where personal supervision of the library's patrons and users is not practical. Marking materials with a property stamp even on rare and special collections materials is necessary to assure identification of stolen materials. The ALA Association of College and Research Libraries Rare Books and Manuscripts Section's Security Committee has an online publication,

"Guidelines for the Security of Rare Books, Manuscripts and Special Collections," that includes information on marking (1999, www. ala.org/ala/acrl/acrlstandards/guidelinesecurity.html). This policy also makes recommendations on security and supervised use of rare materials.

Loss Prevention Resources

Insurance Company Inspections

One of the criteria in choosing an insurance company should be its loss prevention inspection service capabilities and the competence of its staff in loss control and protection. An agreement should be reached with the insurance company for regular inspections and loss control services. The library's insurance company loss prevention engineering services may be particularly valuable when adding to a library, changing its configuration, or changing protection or detection.

Local Fire Department Inspections

Good rapport with the local fire chief is very desirable. The library should invite firefighters to become familiar with the layout of the library building and encourage periodic inspections by members of the fire department and the librarian or his or her designee. It is important to make sure the fire department is aware of and understands the protection system provided and has an effective preplan to respond to a fire.

Fidelity and Crime

Any organization can suffer an employee dishonesty claim. Chances of a claim can be minimized by good accounting practices, including the proper division of responsibilities, such as signature authority for checks, deposit authority, and so on. The library's fidelity and crime insurance company can offer suggestions to minimize the chance of loss.

OSHA Requirements

The Occupational Safety and Health Act (OSHA), adopted by the federal government in 1970, applies to all employees (except state and local government) with reference to employee injuries. Some states have taken over OSHA responsibilities and may apply the regulations to state and local governmental bodies. The most important part of this statute for libraries concerns the maintenance of adequate records relating to on-the-job employee injuries. Details of this record-keeping requirement are contained in the U.S. Department of Labor booklet titled *Record-Keeping Requirements Under the Williams-Steiger Occupational Safety and Health Act of 1970.*

It is the authors' belief that most, if not all, libraries (along with educational facilities) are exempt from OSHA's record-keeping provisions, but not from the law itself. However, good management practice dictates that libraries should maintain internal records of claims, regardless of whether the OSHA requirement applies to them.

Sovereign Immunity

While sovereign immunity may not be a true loss prevention technique, nevertheless, it is a protection in the form of immunity available to many institutions. Virtually all governmental bodies in the United States have some form of governmental immunity. These immunities vary greatly by state and jurisdiction and some have been eroded by court decisions that have weakened their effectiveness as a defense. The library director should be knowledgeable on the issue and inform liability insurers such a defense exists. In some states, the existence of an insurance policy can be considered a waiver of the sovereign immunity defense unless an endorsement is attached to the policy stating this policy does not constitute a waiver of the immunity.

Loss Control for Workers' Compensation

Repetitive Motion Injuries

While libraries are not inherently dangerous, there are patterns of claims that develop from library employees. Of course, any employee can suffer an injury resulting from a slip, trip, or fall (prevention is discussed later under General Liability). However, a pattern of claims common to libraries is repetitive motion injury. These injuries, if undetected, can result in serious damage and often lead to surgery and extensive rehabilitation.

Repetitive motion injuries in libraries arise from two sources: shipping and receiving activities or heavy keyboard activity. Shipping and receiving personnel are generally handling and packaging or unpackaging books on a regular basis. The constant reaching associated with this process can lead to repetitive motion injuries in wrists, arms, and shoulders. To minimize these injuries, the library should ensure the work is examined to determine how the ergonomics of the area can be improved. A visit from the company providing workers' compensation insurance should be able to make recommendations to increase worker safety.

Keyboard-related repetitive motion injuries generally appear as a carpal tunnel injury. To minimize potential for this injury, every workstation should have an ergonomic review. Most workstation furniture and keyboard equipment today have ergonomic features, but, to be effective, the features must be put to use. Often, the equipment manufacturers offer suggestions on ergonomic structure. There also are Web sites that offer guidelines on the subject.

Other Sources of Employee Injuries

Two other common types of injury result from lifting or being struck by falling objects. There are many guidelines available for appropriate lifting technique, which include wearing a lifting harness to support the employee's back. Finally, loose shelving has proven to be the source of employee injury, so all shelving should be anchored in position to prevent claims that result from unstable shelving.

Safeguarding the Public
General Liability

Injuries to library patrons and the public generally fall into the slips, trips, and falls category. These injuries may occur in any location, from the parking lot to the aisles between the books to the freshly washed floors of the lavatories. Libraries, like all businesses open to the public, have an obligation to provide an environment as safe from the potential for injury as possible.

Parking lots should be well lit so that patrons can make their way safely after dark. Stairways, either internal or external, should similarly be well lit and have the requisite handrails for those patrons who need them. It is important after inclement weather to have parking lots and stairs cleared and dried as soon as possible. Aisles and traffic pathways should be kept clear of books, carts, or any other objects that can obstruct free access. Additionally, exit signs should be clearly visible and not blocked by shelving or other equipment.

Automobile Liability

All drivers should practice courteous and safe-driving habits at all times. If the library has employment positions for which driving is a function of the job, it should review driving records annually by ordering a motor vehicle report. Drivers should understand any major moving traffic violation, such as driving under the influence (commonly know as DUI or DWI) or reckless driving, may result in termination, even if these violations did not occur while conducting library business. Additionally, a frequency of less serious violations or accidents (three or more) in a three-year period should also prompt the library to consider suspension or termination. Drivers should periodically be asked to take defensive driver training instruction. Such courses can be found through the National Safety Council (www.nsc.org).

Appendix E provides a sample library safety inspection checklist.

Directors' and Officers' Liability and Employment Practices Liability

Though loss prevention in these areas is more intangible than that related to preventing physical loss, it is necessary and possible. The board should be provided with a manual that includes, but is not limited to, the mission and the ethics of the governing body or community, the board's responsibility to the community, and the administrative business rules of the library. While the Sarbanes-Oxley Act of 2002, which introduced new financial practices and corporate governance regulations, may not legally apply to a library, the intent of the act should be adopted.

Relative to employment practice issues, appropriate policies that recognize and protect the rights of employees as spelled out by federal and state law are a minimum. Managers and supervisors should be trained accordingly, and employee issues requiring disciplinary action or termination must be specifically and appropriately documented. Complaints of sexual harassment must be dealt with promptly and objectively. Failure to do so can result in expensive, embarrassing, and tedious litigation.

CHAPTER 5
Risk Financing

After identifying and quantifying the exposures that threaten the library's assets, and reducing the potential for losses through preventive measures, such as sprinkler systems, improved housekeeping practices, or preventive maintenance of key equipment, the library will still experience losses, albeit less frequently and with less severity than would be the case without implementing loss-prevention measures. Therefore, it is still necessary for the library to have a financial plan so that it can continue to function and provide uninterrupted service to its constituents despite adverse situations. This step in the process is referred to as risk financing and is accomplished in one of several ways:

- non-insurance transfers;
- self-insurance; or
- purchase of commercial insurance.

Non-insurance Transfers

The primary purpose of a non-insurance transfer is to prevent the library from being responsible for losses that arise out of the operations of others with whom it does business. A non-insurance transfer is accomplished by an indemnity or hold harmless clause in a contract or lease agreement. In essence, it is an agreement whereby the third party with whom the library is contracting agrees to hold the library harmless from any and all claims that arise out of that party's operations. Because the third party has agreed to hold the library harmless, that party will then absorb the financial costs of any claim made against the library as a result of its operations.

For example, the library should use an indemnity clause in construction contracts whereby the contractor assumes all liability for accidents to workers and others arising from the construction. In the event a patron of the library is injured as a result of the construction, the contractor will assume responsibility for any financial loss the library may incur from this claim.

Lease agreements are another area where the transfer of risk to another party may be the most appropriate risk-financing method. A lease relating to computer or photocopying equipment, for example, may be worded so the manufacturer or owner of the equipment is responsible for loss of or damage to the equipment, particularly if the manufacturer or owner is responsible for maintaining the equipment.

It is conceivable that a third party could be negligent for a claim causing damage in excess of the assets of the third party, rendering any indemnity agreement ineffective. For this reason, when a non-insurance transfer is used, the third party (vendor, owner, contractor, or others) should be required by the contract to provide the library with evidence it has insurance for its operations. Further, the library should require that it be named as an additional insured on the other party's liability insurance policy. This will provide the library with a greater likelihood that the contracting party is able to meet the financial obligations that may result if a claim is made as a result of the other party's operations.

Self-insurance

Self-insurance is frequently confused with a lack of insurance in the event of a loss. But there is an important difference. A library that does not purchase insurance and then suffers an uninsured loss must find the funds to pay for that uninsured loss itself. The library may have to scramble in order to deal with the financial consequences of the uninsured loss. Depending on the size of the loss, this may involve a special budget appropriation, bond issue, or the need to divert other resources in order to pay for the damages resulting from the loss.

Conversely, self-insurance is a risk management tool. It is a conscious decision to accept the financial consequences of certain risks once those risks have been identified and quantified. Self-insurance is usually accomplished through a budget-line item known as a self-insurance reserve. Funds will be allocated to the self-insurance reserve from each year's budget. The amount allocated each year will depend upon the previously completed risk quantification process. Funds in the self-insurance reserve should be adequate to cover anticipated losses that the library has decided to retain rather than insure. In the case of large self-insured retention (SIR), it may be necessary to retain the services of an actuary or other consultant to advise the library regarding appropriate amounts to be budgeted to the self-insurance reserve each year. These amounts can then be used to pay for claims that fall within insurance policy deductibles, and for claims for risks on which the library chooses to self-insure and not purchase insurance.

The library should self-insure those risks that:

- are so small in amount as to present no financial hardship. Examples include loss of books in the possession of individual borrowers, damage to vehicles in the library's parking lot, or goodwill medical payments for small injuries due to slips and falls; and
- occur with high frequency and low severity or with reasonable certainty and predictability so that the probable total annual loss can be projected for budgeting purposes. In such cases, the premium for insurance will probably exceed the predictable losses (for example, loss of books due to theft or vandalism). In some instances, as in the case of automobile collision insurance, the library can reduce its premium cost by assuming a reasonable deductible or retention per loss.

The library should insure all other risks that can be insured (that is, which are of an insurable nature). This will involve the design and purchase of an insurance program that will allow for the retention of small and predictable losses and the transfer of large losses that could have adverse financial consequences. The next chapter contains an extensive discussion of insurance coverage. However, before exploring the lines of insurance coverage, the library should become familiar with available professional assistance resources that aid the selection of commercial insurance purchases and products.

Professional Assistance

The professional assistance the librarian needs in handling the insurance program may come from one or more of the sources described below.

Risk Manager

If the library is large or is part of a large institution (such as a university) or entity (such as a state or county), its risk and insurance management program may be administered by a professional risk manager. In these situations, librarians should consider themselves an integral part of the risk management process. While the system risk manager will usually make insurance decisions, the librarian should be familiar with insurance policies purchased to protect the library's assets.

Consultant

An insurance consultant (either an individual or a firm that specializes in risk and insurance management consulting) may be engaged to assist in the risk management process, either in its entirety, or specifically related to the risk financing part of the process. A consultant may be retained on a continuing basis to act on behalf of the library in the capacity of professional risk manager. A consultant also may be engaged periodically to do specific projects, such as review insurance risks and lines of coverage, prepare specifications for bidding, or to assist in loss settlements.

The primary need for an insurance consultant will occur when the library wants an independent and objective survey of its risks and lines of coverage, when it wants to request proposals for insurance brokerage services, or when it desires to secure proposals for its various lines of insurance coverage. Soliciting proposals, either for insurance brokerage services or for lines of coverage, may be by directive of the board of trustees, at the discretion of the person in the library responsible for the insurance program, or, in some cases, by a statutory requirement for public entities to do so periodically. In any event, if the library does not have a professional risk manager, it may wish to tap the services of an insurance consultant for drafting specifications for brokerage services and making recommendations as to insurance markets from which bids should be requested.

To prepare the specifications, the consultant must be thoroughly familiar with the operations of the library and with the risks to which it is subject. The consultant must be available to analyze proposals when they are received to determine whether they conform to the specifications and then submit a recommendation as to which proposals should be accepted, along with supporting documentation as to the reasons for the recommendation.

Generally, proposals for insurance brokerage services and insurance coverage should be sought no more frequently than every three to five years, depending on a number of factors. These include satisfaction with the current agent or broker and incumbent insurance companies, the capabilities of those providing risk and insurance management services to the library, and insurance market conditions. If the library is satisfied with the performance of the current agent or broker and insurance companies, barring a statutory requirement for bidding, there is no reason to upset those relationships. However, from time to time, it is worth entertaining some competition, if for no other reason than to know what other options might be available to the library. It should be noted that it usually will be difficult to persuade the better insurance markets to consider providing coverage if the library's programs are sent out to bid more frequently than every three to five years, or if the library changes insurers often.

The consultant will require a fee, which will be negotiated with the library. Depending on the services the library requires and the length of the engagement, the fee may be an annual retainer based on the actual time spent on the account, or a project fee agreed upon by the library and the consultant.

Agent or Broker

Most libraries, especially those without a full-time risk manager, will work with an insurance agent or broker who will be charged with providing professional advice and service and placing the library's insurance.

Generally, the insurance agent represents the insurance company and the insurance broker represents the library. However, the agent who is in the category known as an independent agent represents many companies and will act on behalf of the insured, much as a broker. Only in certain limited instances, such as binding coverage, collecting premiums, and issuing policies or endorsements, will he or she be an agent of the insurance company; as a rule, these activities will not interfere with his or her acting on behalf of the library.

A number of insurance companies operate with exclusive or captive agents; for example, agents who are not permitted to represent any other company. Such agents generally will not be able to operate in a legal relationship as agents of the library.

The broker or independent agent normally will have a number of companies from which he or she can secure premium quotations for the library's insurance program. If the library has not retained a consultant, a broker or agent will work with the library to draw up specifications and secure quotations from a number of insurance companies at regular intervals, usually as noted above, every three to five years.

Occasionally, the library may subject the program or parts of the program (for example, only some of the lines of coverage or some policies) to competition from other brokers or agents. The library administration should be mindful of the benefit of long-term relationships and stability in the insurance program, however. For this reason, incumbent agents, brokers, and insurers should only be replaced when there is a significant benefit to the library, either in terms of broader coverage, better service, or substantially lower costs. An insurance program should not be changed for a modest cost reduction unless there are other problems with the program, such as poor service or questionable financial integrity of the agent, broker, or underwriter. As noted above, competition should typically be considered only every three to five years unless there are problems with the program or insurance market conditions that create a need for more frequent market competition.

The agent or broker will be compensated either by commissions or by fees. If by commission, the remuneration for the agent or broker will be included in the premium on the policies he or she issued or placed. Commissions are typically charged as a percentage of premium based upon prevailing industry standards. The cost of consultation and professional advice provided by an agent or broker is typically included in the commission compensation structure. Some brokers also provide services on a fee basis, similar to consultants. In that case, the fee will be an amount agreed upon by the library and the agent or broker in the course of their negotiations. Note that the library always should request a report of the sum of all fees, commissions, and profit-sharing that an agent or broker receives on the library's account. A sample request for proposal for insurance brokerage services can be found in appendix G.

Choosing a Consultant, Agent, or Broker

When selecting an insurance consultant, agent, or broker, the library should consider:

- the reputation of the individual or firm in the community where the library is located;
- the individual or firm's relationship with insurance companies;
- the individual or firm's experience in working with libraries, museums, or other similar institutions, and in the field of public or private institutional insurance;
- the general competence and professional training of all individuals who will be working with the library on the assignment—this should include consideration of professional credentials in the risk and insurance management field, such

as Chartered Property Casualty Underwriter (CPCU), Associate in Risk Management (ARM), Certified Risk Manager (CRM), Risk Management for Public Entities (RMPE), and Accredited Adviser in Insurance (AAI);

- the individual or firm's willingness and ability to allocate the personnel and the time necessary to complete the assignment in the time frame required by the library; and
- depending on the library's needs, the specialized resources that the individual or firm can bring to bear for the benefit of the library.

The true value of an insurance policy for the library is the promise of the underwriter to pay for a covered loss. At the time of loss, certain elements become critical. The insurance policies should be properly written, especially pertaining to the property or operations covered and the limit of liability. The name of the insured should be listed correctly. The insurance company must be financially sound, properly licensed, and of good reputation. Choosing a competent consultant, agent, or broker helps the library select an insurance underwriter that will satisfy these criteria.

Services Provided by a Consultant, Agent, or Broker

The consultant, agent, or broker will be engaged to assist the library administration in the performance of the risk management functions for the library. Depending on the scope of the engagement, a consultant may be asked to provide any or all of the following services. Generally, an agent or broker will be expected to:

- assist in risk identification and quantification, including developing values for insurance purposes;
- assist the library administration in its loss prevention efforts;
- analyze risks and review the insurance program periodically (at least annually);
- advise the library regarding appropriate deductibles or self-insurance retentions;
- keep the library apprised of developments in the insurance industry that may impact the library's insurance program;
- periodically test the insurance market to ensure the best program is provided, including the broadest coverage at the best price;
- assist in determining the best value to the library (the program with the lowest premium is not necessarily the best option);

- place and maintain insurance coverage in force with financially sound companies;
- advise the library administration of any changes in the financial integrity or business profile of the underwriters assigned to the library's insurance program;
- be available to consult on changes in operation and on new construction and its effect on the insurance program;
- advise the library on the minimum coverage and liability limits required of third-party contractors and vendors; and
- assist in reporting claims and adjusting losses.

Consultant or Agent or Broker?

The argument is made that only a consultant on a fee basis will possess the objectivity necessary for a professional job. Conversely, the argument continues, an agent or broker compensated by commissions that are a percentage of premium lacks the incentive to reduce premium costs because that would lower his or her own commissions. While this may be true in some rare cases, consultants, agents, and brokers are all professionals and, as such, their work should be judged based on the effectiveness of their services in assisting the library in managing risk and in obtaining comprehensive insurance programs at competitive costs.

There are means of measuring the effectiveness of an agent or broker just as there are of the consultant. Periodically having agents or brokers compete against each other for the library's insurance business will ensure the library has access to the most comprehensive program at the best cost. When this is done, it may be worthwhile to engage the services of a consultant to manage this process if the library does not have qualified staff or the time to complete the analysis necessary to make an informed decision. If the library feels obligated to place insurance with more than one insurance agent or broker, to either maintain competition or to reassure itself it has the best program at the best price, it might engage a consultant to supervise the entire insurance program.

The Library's Involvement

No insurance consultant, agent, or broker can perform satisfactorily without full and complete cooperation of the insured. It is essential that some individual who is thoroughly familiar with the library's operations and plans be available for consultation. Usually, this is the librarian or the chief fiscal officer.

The library board should review the risk and insurance program annually, generally prior to policy expiration. In order to accomplish this, the insurance consultant, broker or agent should arrange to meet with the librarian several months (120 to 180 days) prior to expiration of insurance policies to review changes in the library's operations and exposures and to secure the necessary underwriting information, such as payroll, square footage, and real and personal property values. The effectiveness of the insurance program depends upon the completeness and accuracy of the information supplied by the library. The responsibility of the consultant, agent, or broker for reviewing insurance regularly cannot be met unless he or she has the full cooperation of both the library staff and the board of directors.

It is important to remember, however, the library personnel responsible for this process are ultimately responsible for the decision, and must make the time to be well-informed about the process and available options in order to make the appropriate choice. The library administration still has the ultimate responsibility for the protection of the library's assets; therefore, this responsibility cannot be delegated to a consultant, agent, or broker. In insurance, as in other areas of business and professional services, the quality of services the library receives will depend on the people it chooses to do business with and the library administration's management of those professionals.

Insurance Companies

After risks have been identified and quantified; loss-prevention efforts implemented; risks transferred to others via hold harmless or indemnity agreements; self-insurance decisions made; and consultants, agents, and brokers selected, the library must make risk-financing decisions regarding commercial insurance. Obviously, the main offering from commercial insurance companies is the insurance policies to protect the assets of the library from being lost due to catastrophic occurrences. The next chapter deals with specifics regarding insurance coverage.

In conjunction with their insurance policies, insurance companies also offer other services that supplement the library's own risk management efforts. Generally, these services are included in the premium charged; however, there may be some services that require an additional fee.

Initial Physical Inspections

Working with the library, insurance companies will develop a firsthand knowledge of the risks at the library by conducting on-site assessments of the library's exposures. The information gained will be used in the insurance company's underwriting; it also will supplement the library's own risk analysis and can help in identifying and quantifying exposures so the library can evaluate the most effective risk management techniques for the exposures identified.

Annual Inspection Program

The library should establish a regular inspection program for safety and fire protection purposes. Many insurance companies have loss prevention specialists to provide engineering and inspection services to help the library in developing necessary fire safety inspections. These inspections should help the library identify the vulnerabilities in its properties and operations, and then develop plans to remove or resolve these issues to eliminate or decrease risks.

Recommendations

Especially with regard to the library's property, the insurance company can offer suggestions that, when implemented, may reduce risks of loss of the library's most valuable assets—its collections and building.

Rating Agencies

There are a handful of rating agencies that analyze and publish opinions of insurance companies' financial strength and their ability to meet obligations to policyholders. These opinions are generally offered in the form of ratings published on an annual basis. In the event a company's financial status suddenly changes due to some unforeseen circumstance, such as a catastrophic insured event or a sudden increase in loss reserves, revised ratings may be issued. The ratings have a key that indicates both the size and the financial strength of the company. The oldest of the rating agencies are A. M. Best Company and Standard & Poor's. The library's consultant, agent, or broker should help set a minimum standard rating for acceptable insurers, but generally not less than A-minus.

CHAPTER 6
Risk Financing—Insurance

Most libraries will buy the following types of insurance coverage:

- real and personal property, including library collections, fine arts, rare books, and valuable papers;
- boiler and machinery;
- workers' compensation;
- general liability;
- automobile liability and physical damage;
- umbrella or excess liability;
- directors', trustees', and officers' liability;
- public officials' liability;
- crime and employee dishonesty;
- fiduciary liability; and
- employee benefits liability.

For larger libraries and systems, each of the lines of coverage listed above is usually underwritten on a separate policy. Coverage may be underwritten by the same company under different policies or by different companies specializing in certain types of risk (such as property underwriters, casualty underwriters).

For a small or mid-size library, one insurance company may insure the entire library, with the exception of coverage for fine arts and special collections, which may be underwritten by specialty insurers. For smaller libraries, several of these coverage lines (property, general liability, automobile liability) may be purchased together under what is known as a package policy. The package policy may include a variety of insurance coverage, depending on the underwriting practices of the particular company. There may be some premium savings with the package. In a package policy, the premium is the sum of the individual coverage premium to which a package policy credit is applied. A package policy will generally provide a premium savings because the administrative costs are reduced for the insurance company if two or more lines of coverage are included. Larger libraries may still find, however, separate policies written through different companies and different agents and brokers may sometimes be more economical and more desirable than a single package policy. Which option is better will depend on the insurance market as well as what the insurance companies in a particular market are willing to underwrite and offer.

The Insurance Policy

Insurance policies, whether a package policy or stand-alone policies for individual lines of coverage, are constructed the same way and have five major components.

Declarations

Policy declarations state basic information about the policy, such as:

- the named insured and mailing address;
- the policy period;
- the amount of coverage;
- the locations, property, and operations covered;
- policy premium; and
- policy deductibles.

Insuring Agreements

In this section, the library will find information specific to the insurance to be provided, including:

- coverage clauses that spell out what property, operations, and activities are covered;
- definitions of important terms used in the policy;
- policy territory;
- explanation of how limits of coverage apply;
- valuation of property covered; and
- defense obligations of the insurance company.

Exclusions

This section, as its name implies, enumerates property, operations, and activities that are not intended to be covered by the policy.

Policy Conditions

This section of the policy contains general conditions not related to the specifics of policy coverage, such as:

- conditions that void coverage;
- the insured's duties in the event of a loss;
- requirements for filing proof of loss;
- other insurance clauses that spell out how the insurance will apply in the event more than one policy applies to a loss covered under a particular policy;
- subrogation rights, which are the rights of the insurance company to pursue recovery from a third party for a covered claim;
- policy assignment rights; and
- cancellation clause.

Endorsements

This section of the policy contains any changes agreed to by the insured and the insurance company that amend the standard policy in ways that make the policy more tailored to the needs of a particular insured party.

To determine whether a particular property, operation, or activity is covered, the library should first review the insuring agreements to see if that property, operation, or activity is included in the coverage clauses. Next, it should check the exclusions to see if there are any listed that would be applicable to the circumstance the library is considering. Finally, the library should check the policy endorsements to see if either the insuring agreements or exclusions have been modified in any way that is applicable to the circumstance for which it is seeking coverage.

Property Insurance

In designing a property insurance program, it is important the policy be broad enough to respond to claims for damage to all property owned, leased, or in the care, custody, and control of the insured. Further, it is important the policy be broad enough to cover damage from a wide variety of perils. (Refer to chapter 2.) The property policy covering the library should cover all property and perils identified under Property Insured and Covered Perils in this chapter. The amount of coverage should be sufficient to cover the property owned, leased, or in the care, custody, and control of the library. All locations owned by the library should be listed on the property policy. In addition, all locations the library leases, and that it is responsible for insuring, also should be listed.

Limits of Liability

Blanket Policy

Most library property coverage will be written to provide blanket coverage, for example, an insurance policy or policy form covering more than one type of property or multiple locations in a single amount or limit of liability. For example, a blanket form covering library property may be written for a single amount of insurance and cover all buildings owned by the library as well as the contents of those buildings, including furniture and fixtures, equipment, books, library materials, and other tangible property. A blanket policy is desirable because it permits different types of properties at various locations to be included in a single policy with a single amount of insurance. This simplifies administration of the library's property insurance program because all property owned by the library is covered by one policy with a blanket amount of insurance. The library does not have to worry that an individual piece of property is underinsured.

If the library submits an annual statement of values (SOV), most property underwriters will offer a blanket policy. The library's SOV should provide the underwriter with a list of all the buildings to be insured, and the best estimate of the replacement cost of each. Replacement cost is defined as the cost to rebuild the entire structure at current prices if it were totally destroyed. The library also should include an estimate of the replacement cost of the contents of the building. Again, this is what it would cost to replace the entire contents of the library at current prices if everything were destroyed in one loss.

Items need not be listed individually. Rather, an estimate of the total cost to replace all library contents is what is required. This includes both general and special collections. The replacement cost for the collections should be included with a list of the contents of each library building. (Refer to chapter 3 for a discussion on establishing the replacement cost of library collections.)

The library need only file an SOV annually, unless it makes significant changes, such as the acquisition of a new building or other property. The SOV is typically filed at the beginning of the policy period.

Some insurance policies will be written with what is known as coinsurance. A coinsurance clause requires the values reported be equal to a certain percentage of the replacement cost, typically 80 percent, 90 percent, or 100 percent. In the event of a loss, the library and the insurance company will become coinsurers if the values reported are determined to be less than the required coinsurance percentage, an amount equal to the percentage that values were underreported. If, for example, a policy requires 100 percent coinsurance and, at the time of a loss, it is determined values are only equal to 90 percent of the full replacement cost values, the library will be a coinsurer for 10 percent of the loss. Whenever possible it is recommended that reported values equal 100 percent of the replacement cost and coinsurance clauses be deleted by endorsement.

Even on a policy with blanket limits of liability, there are some lines of coverage that will be provided at a lower limit than the blanket limit. A number of coverage types will be underwritten with a lower limit, known as a sublimit. The most important of these coverage types for the library are fine arts, valuable papers, and rare books. These are often insured on a separate policy underwritten by a company that specializes in providing coverage only for these types of collections. These items may, however, be included in the blanket property policy. In either case, the underwriter usually requires a list of individual items to be insured with a value assigned to each item. The value assigned may be an actual appraisal value or it may be the librarian's estimate of the market value or replacement cost (if indeed the item could be replaced) of any particular piece of the collection.

Whatever value the librarian assigns will usually become the insured value and the valuation clause of the policy will be written on what is known as a stated value or an agreed value. The wording for the insured value of these items may read "as per schedule on file with the company" (meaning the insurance company), "as per schedule submitted by the insured," or "as per schedule on file with the insured." Other lines of coverage that may be underwritten with a sublimit typically include property in transit, EDP media, accounts receivable, flood and surface water, earthquake, and terrorism.

When new buildings or new properties are added, the coverage may be handled in a number of different ways. Many blanket policies provide some period of time of automatic coverage for such properties. For example, the policy may provide that new properties acquired by the insured are automatically covered, subject to some limit of liability (a sublimit, usually less than the blanket policy limit) for a certain period of time (such as thirty or sixty days) even though they are not reported immediately to the insurance company. Before the time period for the automatic coverage has elapsed, the library must report the new property to the insurance company, along with information about the building, including its construction, protection, occupancy, exposure, and replacement cost. Some policies may require the library to submit all underwriting information regarding a new property before coverage will be bound by the underwriter. What is important is that the library knows the requirement under the policy.

Schedule Policy

Some policies, particularly for smaller libraries, may be written on a scheduled basis. In this policy form, each location owned by the library is listed and a value, or amount of insurance, is provided for each location based on the values submitted by the library. The potential pitfall of this approach is that if a location is insured for an amount that is less than the true replacement cost, the library's loss will be limited to the scheduled, or insured, limit of liability for that particular location. In a blanket policy, on the other hand, the total limit of liability is available for each location insured on the policy.

Deductibles

Deductibles are amounts, or parts of losses, that will be absorbed by the library in the event of a loss. Generally, the amount of a policy deductible varies with the size of the library and its budget. Because the deductible represents an amount of loss that the insurance company will not pay, premium credits are provided in return for the library's agreement to accept deductibles. The higher the deductible, the greater the premium credit the library will receive. A small library may readily accept a $1,000 or $2,500 deductible, especially if experience indicates it is not likely to have more than one or two losses in a given year. Similarly, a larger library may consider absorbing a deductible that is multiple times those, and a very large system may be able to accept deductibles as high as $100,000 or more. Whether a higher deductible is desirable will depend on the financial position of the library, its past and expected loss experience, and the amount of premium credit.

Cancellation Clause

Every policy contains a cancellation clause that allows either party to cancel the insurance contract with a certain amount of prior written notice to the other party. Most policies provide for thirty days' prior written notice by the insurance company. However, many insurance companies will agree to longer periods for prior notice of cancellation—sixty days' notice—if requested. The one exception is for nonpayment of premium. In this instance, most insurers reserve the right to cancel the policy with only ten days' notice.

If the insurance company cancels coverage the premium earned will be a pro-rata amount of the annual premium based on the number of days coverage was in effect. However, if the library requests cancellation, a short-rate penalty will apply. This means premium paid will be more than would have been paid on a pro-rata basis.

Other Insurance

Because the basic premise of insurance is the insured should be made whole after a loss, but should not profit from a loss, every policy contains what is known as an other insurance clause. This clause determines how the policy will pay in the event there is more than one policy covering any property. In this way, the insured cannot collect from more than one insurance company such that the recovery will be more than the value of the insured property that is lost or damaged.

The other insurance clause will designate the coverage the insurance company will provide:

- primary coverage—it will be the first one to pay in the event of a loss;
- excess coverage—it will pay only after limits of liability provided by any other policy have already been paid, and the insured has not yet been made whole for the lost property; or
- contributory coverage—it will pay based on a pro-rata share with other coverage in effect for the same property. In this case, each policy will pay based on the percentage its limit of liability bears to the total limit of liability purchased to cover the property that has been damaged or lost.

Property Insured

The property covered may include any or all of the following:

Real property
- buildings, including all buildings owned or leased by the library, or those under construction;
- permanently installed machinery and equipment; and
- landscaping.

Personal property
- furniture and fixtures;
- supplies and materials;
- books and library materials, including periodicals, manuscripts, card catalogues, shelf lists, films, prints, audio and video tapes, recordings, digital facsimiles, cameras, projection equipment, musical instruments and related and similar equipment and accessories, drawings, artwork, fine arts, valuable papers and records, rare books, and all other materials intended for the use of library patrons;
- machinery and equipment, including computers;
- EDP media;
- accounts receivable;
- improvement and betterments in buildings in which the library is a tenant; and
- property of others in the library's care, custody, or control, which includes property of the library's employees. This also may include a large variety of property, such as books on loan, office machines, microfilming equipment, copy machines, microform readers and printers, scanners, digital cameras, and other equipment. The responsibility of the library for these items should be clearly stated in the loan or lease agreement or contract related to the equipment.

Some of the property listed above may be excluded by the basic policy. However, it generally can be added to the list of covered property by endorsement. Other property (such as valuable papers and records and rare books) may be covered by the policy, but may be subject to more limited coverage both in terms of limits or amount of coverage provided, and causes of loss for which the property may be insured, which may be more limited than for other library property.

Property Excluded

Covered property usually does not include any or all of the following:

- accounts, bills, currency, deeds, evidences of debt;
- animals;
- excavations;
- foundations;

- land;
- underground pipes, flues, or drains;
- vehicles;
- aircraft; and
- watercraft.

Covered Perils

The policy may be written on either an all-risk or a named-peril basis. An all-risk policy insures the library against damage due to all risk of physical loss except those perils specifically excluded. A named-peril policy insures against losses from specifically named perils. Most policies are written on an all-risk basis because it provides broader coverage for the library. When seeking competitive quotations from various insurers, the library should always include a request for a proposal on a property policy underwritten on an all-risk basis.

Following is a list of perils insured against by most property policies:

- fire and lightning;
- riot or civil commotion;
- explosion;
- vehicle damage;
- smoke;
- hail;
- aircraft damage;
- wind (including hurricanes and tornados);
- vandalism and malicious mischief;
- sprinkler leakage;
- water damage from defective plumbing, heating, and air-conditioning systems;
- collapse of buildings or structures;;
- glass breakage;
- burglary, theft, robbery;
- boiler and machinery; and
- property in transit.

An all-risk policy will include many of the above perils. However, coverage for some perils, such as property in transit or glass breakage, may be subject to a sublimit that is lower than the policy limit. Further, as noted above, it will exclude certain uninsurable perils, such as wear and tear, gradual deterioration, mechanical breakdown, erasure of magnetic recordings due to electrical or magnetic disturbance or errors in processing, inherent vice, loss due to dampness or dryness of atmosphere, changes in temperature, mold (unless it is the direct result of an insured peril), marring or scratching, loss through dishonesty of persons to whom the property is entrusted, and certain catastrophes, among which are flood and surface water, earthquake, war, and nuclear damage.

Flood

Flood insurance may not be available from the library's insurance company, especially for a facility located in a designated flood zone. For that reason, the federal government offers what is known as the National Flood Insurance Program (NFIP), which enables property owners in participating communities to purchase insurance protection against losses from flooding. Participation in NFIP is based on an agreement between local communities and the federal government that states if a community will adopt and enforce a floodplain management ordinance to reduce future flood risks to new construction in special flood hazard areas, the federal government will make flood insurance available within the community as a financial protection against flood losses.

NFIP is administered by the Federal Emergency Management Agency (FEMA). The flood insurance policy is limited in amount and is not subject to endorsement or modification. Coverage is provided for buildings and contents, both on an actual cash value basis. Replacement cost coverage is not available. The maximum limit of liability available as of this writing is $500,000 per building for real property and $500,000 per building for contents. However, no coverage is provided for any property located in a basement other than building service equipment. A local insurance agent can determine whether the library's community is eligible and can quote rates and premium under the program.

Given the limited amount of insurance available under NFIP, libraries with greater values exposed to flooding may want to ask their property insurer if they would be willing to provide some additional flood coverage in excess of that provided by NFIP. This coverage can usually be provided for an additional premium.

Earthquake/Earth Movement

Coverage for earth movement, which includes earthquake, landslides, mudflow, earth sinking, earth rising or shifting, and volcanic eruption, can be added to the policy. An additional premium will be charged for this coverage, which is typically subjected to a larger deductible than other lines of coverage on the policy.

Terrorism

The Terrorism Risk Insurance Act of 2002 (TRIA) was passed to establish a temporary federal program to provide a system of shared public and private compensation for insured losses resulting from acts of terrorism. TRIA requires all insurance companies that offer property and casualty insurance policies must make property and casualty insurance coverage for losses resulting from terrorism available on terms and conditions that do not differ materially from the general policy terms and conditions. As a result, every insurer offering the library a property policy must offer the option to purchase terrorism coverage as part of the policy. There is an extra premium charge for terrorism coverage. TRIA is set to expire at the end of 2005 and it is not known, at this time, what coverage for terrorism will be available beyond that date.

Additional Lines of Coverage

All policies exclude coverage for certain types of property and for loss by certain perils. The library may delete some exclusions by endorsement. However, there typically is a premium charge when exclusions are deleted because coverage is being added and a premium must be paid for any additional coverage. The insurance agent or consultant should review policy exclusions and limitations in light of the library's needs and discuss available coverage extensions with the librarian, risk manager, or the business officer responsible for the purchase of insurance for the library. Some of the following additional lines of coverage are part of the basic property policy; others may not be included in the basic policy. However, they are important types of coverage and can be added to the policy by endorsement.

Debris Removal

As its name implies, this coverage pays to remove debris caused by a covered loss. This coverage is typically part of the basic property policy.

Demolition and Increased Cost of Construction (D&ICC)/ Building Ordinance or Law.

New construction and renovation typically must conform to local and state building codes. When a building is damaged as a result of a fire or other insured peril, a library built in accordance with building codes in effect at the time of the original construction may be required either to be demolished or to be rebuilt to conform to codes in effect at the time of the loss. D&ICC coverage, also known as building ordinance or law coverage, available by endorsement to a property policy, will provide coverage for these situations. This endorsement provides coverage if the undamaged portion of the library is required by ordinance to be torn down. It also pays for the increased cost of reconstruction to make the damaged or undamaged portion of the building conform to the requirements of the building and zoning laws.

Temporary Removal of Property/Preservation of Property

Included as part of the basic property policy, this provides coverage for insured or covered property at premises other than the insured building if the property has been moved to a temporary location as a result of a loss at an insured location (in order to protect or preserve it from loss).

EDP Media

Many library records and indexes are maintained on magnetic tapes and disks. Coverage under this section of the policy usually is restricted to the cost of blank media and the cost to reproduce the data from the previous generation of backup data. If backup data is not available, the typical recovery will be the cost of blank media only. Coverage may be extended by endorsement for the cost to replace or restore the lost information when duplicates do not exist. This extension of coverage is subject to a sublimit and an additional premium will be charged.

Property in Transit or Property Off Premises

Property is generally covered at locations described on the policy or within a certain distance of the insured property. If library property will be away from the premises, as in mobile units or temporarily on loan in substantial amounts subject to a single loss, it is desirable to extend the policy. Some coverage can be provided for property in transit and at locations away from the insured premises. This coverage typically is underwritten with a sublimit, a limit of coverage less than blanket policy limit. This will require an estimate of total values at risk and may require a list of locations where the property is usually kept. Coverage will apply while the property is at a temporary location and during transit. Coverage for transit is usually limited to the United States. Therefore, if international transit is anticipated, it is important to ensure the policy is not limited to the United States, and, if it is, to determine the likely value of international shipments and request additional coverage as necessary.

Valuation in the Event of a Loss

Traditionally, the standard fire (property) policy was insured only to the extent of actual cash value (ACV) of the property. This meant property was insured for its replacement cost, less depreciation. Today, such coverage is rarely considered adequate. Instead, coverage typically is purchased on a replacement-cost basis with no deduction for depreciation, as long as the property is replaced. The basic policy often still includes ACV valuation. However, replacement cost is typically included by endorsement. This usually will apply to all buildings and contents insured under the policy, including buildings, fixtures and equipment, and books and library materials. Books common to the typical public library collection are not available on the used book market to a significant extent. In the event of damage or destruction, replacement with new materials will be highly desirable. Such replacement will be at new, not used, prices, and replacement cost coverage will be required to adequately cover the loss.

When coverage is written on a replacement cost basis, a loss adjustment will be made on an ACV basis if the library decides not to repair or replace the property destroyed or damaged during the loss. Some library buildings are designated as historic properties. If this is the case, it is important for the library to discuss the loss valuation clause on the policy with the insurance company. Where historic properties are the subject of the insurance, the policy should be endorsed to provide historic reproduction if that is required. This may require the library to have a recent appraisal, so the library and insurance company have an accurate idea of the value at risk, as well as an understanding before a loss as to what will be involved in restoring the property after a loss.

Special collections, fine arts, valuable papers, and rare books, however, are usually not written on a replacement cost basis, but rather, are insured based on the stated value the library has included on the SOVs and provided to the insurance company (see below for further discussion).

Books and Library Materials

Two methods of insuring books and library materials are most commonly employed.

Blanket Contents Form

Under this coverage, books and library materials are treated as contents, together with furniture, fixtures, and equipment, and insured under the blanket policy form as discussed previously. All insurance companies will insure books and library materials on a replacement cost basis subject to the standard limitation that replacement cost is not recoverable unless the property is actually replaced. If not replaced, the loss will be paid on an ACV (depreciated value) basis. Loss settlement is usually made on the basis of the value of each individual book damaged or destroyed, although the adjuster and the library may agree to an average value per volume when a large number of volumes are involved.

Valuable Papers Form

This form may be used for the library's entire collection or for certain library materials the library considers to be more valuable than those in its general collections. These are usually materials that are unique and cannot be replaced. Special collections may be insured as valuable papers. It is important to note most property (fire) insurance forms limit loss recovery on written and printed records to the cost of the paper plus cost of transcribing or copying the records when there is a duplicate available. Coverage under the valuable papers form is usually subject to the following conditions:

- it provides very broad (all risk) coverage;
- it is not subject to a coinsurance clause;
- it reimburses the insured for the cost to research, replace, restore, or reconstruct records that are damaged or destroyed; and
- the form requires the insured declare unit values for various classes of property (this restriction can be a serious limitation at the time of loss settlement if an appropriate amount of insurance has not been declared for each item).

Either of the two forms should adequately cover the risks of loss. The blanket form allows for the greatest flexibility because the library is neither committed to, nor limited to, a specific value on each book or category of books, nor to a total value of all books and library materials. In a blanket policy, the policy limit of liability applies to the entire property value, building, and contents, including books and other library materials. In the valuable papers form, the amount of insurance applies only to books and library materials. If these are accurately valued, there is no disadvantage to using these forms.

Rare Books, Fine Arts, and Valuable Papers

Property in these categories should always be identified with a specific or stated value for each item (or group of similar items). Generally, such items have an intrinsic value greater than the purchase price. Rare books, valuable papers and records, and fine arts are appropriately insured on a stated valued basis; that is, with a scheduled value for each item for which value will be the basis of loss settlement. This may be in a separate policy or it may be an endorsement to a blanket, or package, policy.

The values may be the original costs, the value set by the librarian, or the value determined by a recognized appraiser. Rarely will the original cost of such items make the library whole in the event of a loss. In other words, the loss settlement on this basis will not be equal to the value of the asset the library has lost based on the current value of the asset. Short of an appraisal, another solution is for the librarian to establish a value for these items, submit the list to the underwriter, and establish an agreed value.

When an item is irreplaceable and there is no ready market for similar items, the value may be purely arbitrary and may depend on whether the proposed value is reasonable and how much premium the library is willing to pay for insurance. By insuring such items on a valued policy or agreed amount form, the insurance company accepts the stated value as the amount of loss if the item is stolen, damaged, or destroyed. It should be noted, however, that the agreed value or replacement cost is the measure of the loss only if the items cannot be restored.

By definition, rare literature is difficult, if not impossible, to replace. As such, in the event of a loss, replacement with a pre-established dollar amount will never fully replace the unique asset that has been destroyed. For that reason, it is critical to focus on protection rather than insurance for these library assets.

Time-Element Coverage

In addition to coverage for the direct damage to the library's property (building and contents), the property policy can be endorsed to provide coverage for what is known as consequential loss, or the loss resulting from damage to the insured's property. Damage or destruction of the library's facilities could disrupt revenue flow, cause a direct loss of income or increase operating costs. The intent of time-element insurance is to place the library in the same position it would have been in had no loss occurred. The term "time element" refers to losses incurred due to the passage of time. The major lines of time-element coverage for a library to consider are:

- Business interruption, which covers the loss of income sustained as a result of a covered loss, and provides coverage for continuing fixed expenses incurred by the library during the period of restoration. These expenses could include sales of used books, and cafeteria or coffee shop sales, for example.
- Extra expense, which covers those additional costs, over and above normal operating costs, that are necessary to re-establish normal operations after a loss. Examples include overtime for non-exempt staff, expedited delivery of equipment, additional costs for inter-library loans, and rental of EDP equipment.
- Expediting expense, which provides for the extra cost incurred on either temporary repairs or overtime labor costs, and the cost to expedite permanent repairs.
- Rental income, which provides coverage for rental fees the library is unable to collect from a tenant in a building owned by the library due to a loss from an insured peril.
- Leasehold interest, which provides coverage for the library in the event the premises it leases are damaged due to a covered peril, and the library must rent other space at an increased cost. Leasehold interest insurance provides coverage for the additional rent the library must pay at the new location.

Boiler and Machinery Coverage

Boilers, machinery and other equipment may be covered by the property policy. However, in the event they are excluded, a separate boiler and machinery (B&M) policy may be required. B&M insurance provides coverage for mechanical, electrical or pressure failure of any equipment that is not excluded. B&M covers boilers, pressure vessels, refrigerating systems, engines, turbines, air tanks, furnaces, generators, motors, and cogeneration plants.

The insurance company provides professional inspection services required by state law. These inspections fulfill a twofold purpose. First, inspectors are licensed by the state (or municipality) and their inspections satisfy the inspection requirements of the state or municipal code. In some instances, it may be required—in other instances it is desirable—to insure hot-water boilers (even though a hot-water boiler explosion is not excluded under the property policy); the insurance company inspection can be used to satisfy the governmental inspection requirements for this type of heating plant. Second, these inspectors are trained engineers. In addition to satisfying legal requirements for inspections, they assist in the library's loss prevention efforts by inspecting boilers, machinery and other equipment to search for evidence of faulty conditions or mechanical weakness. This enables the library to fix potentially dangerous situations before a loss occurs.

Comprehensive B&M coverage is available on a replacement cost basis. The policy covers equipment breakdown and provides property damage coverage (for loss to the damaged boilers or other equipment), business interruption, extra expense, and other consequential damages resulting from the loss to the boiler, machinery, or other equipment.

Crime/Employee Dishonesty

Crime coverage may be purchased either under a comprehensive crime policy, or as individual coverage in the event the library does not feel the need for a comprehensive crime policy. Smaller libraries that purchase a package policy that includes property, liability and boiler and machinery coverage also may include crime coverage. The comprehensive crime policy may include coverage for the following situations.

Employee Dishonesty

This insurance protects the library against loss resulting from the dishonesty of library employees. Loss of money, securities, or other property as a result of fraud, forgery, embezzlement, or theft is covered. As noted above, this coverage may be purchased separately if there is no need for the additional crime coverage. This coverage, also known as fidelity insurance, may be purchased on a blanket basis, which is most common. In this case, coverage is provided for all library employees (all employees are bonded). Library volunteers who handle money also may be included in a blanket bond. Or the coverage may be purchased on a more limited basis either to cover specific individuals or specific positions, such as a treasurer or controller. The Employee Retirement Income and Securities Act (ERISA) requires trustees of the library's pension plans be covered by a fidelity bond.

Theft, Disappearance, and Destruction

This coverage protects the library against the loss of money and securities both on and off library premises, such as while in the custody of a messenger service. Some coverage for money and securities is usually included in the property policy. However, this coverage is typically subject to a sublimit, and the additional coverage provided by the comprehensive crime policy may be needed to provide adequate limits of liability, especially for a large library.

Depositor's Forgery

This insurance protects the library in the event checks or drafts drawn on the library's account are forged or altered by employees or others.

Computer Fraud

This coverage protects the library from the loss of money, securities, and other property due to the theft of that property directly related to the use of any computer to fraudulently cause a transfer of that property from inside the premises to a person other than a messenger outside the premises or to a place outside those premises.

Property Insurance Rates

Rates for commercial, industrial, and public buildings are based on individual features of construction, occupancy, protection, and exposure, known in the insurance industry as COPE factors. Insurance rates vary from one insurance company to the next and may be adjusted by the insurance company following a personal inspection of each building prior to binding coverage. The library often can obtain reduced rates by making improvements in construction, physical protection, and other loss-prevention efforts described in chapter 4.

In most cases, insurance companies have some flexibility in rating. Where premium is substantial, the library's actual loss experience will be important.

Commercial General Liability

While there is a standardized commercial general liability policy form published by the Insurance Service Office (ISO), there are many variations of this form in use by insurance companies. The discussions following are, therefore, only general descriptions of the coverage typically included in these types of policies. The risk management consultant, broker, or agent will advise the library on the specifics of coverage upon placing the coverage with an insurer.

Liability insurance is intended to protect the insured against claims for injuries to persons or property arising out of negligence (his or her torts, further defined as his or her wrongful acts or omissions). Generally, it applies to the unintentional tort of negligence, although coverage also is available where the act is intentional, but the injury unintended.

Bodily Injury

This coverage is intended to apply to injuries to third persons arising as a result of negligence of the library, its employees, or agents. The term "bodily injury" includes death. (Employee injuries fall within workers' compensation statutes and policies.)

Personal Injury

A broader term than bodily injury, includes certain additional torts that are listed in the standard liability forms as follows:

- false arrest, detention or imprisonment, or malicious prosecution;
- libel, slander, defamation, or violation of right of privacy; and
- wrongful entry, eviction, or other invasion of right of privacy.

The standard personal injury endorsement excludes coverage for claims made against the library by employees. This coverage will be discussed later in this chapter, under Employment Practices Liability. Personal injury coverage can be purchased as a stand-alone policy or as an endorsement to the directors' and officers' liability policy.

Property Damage

This refers to the library's liability for damage to property of others caused by the negligence of the library, its employees, or agents. This is especially important if the library building is located in a congested area and where a negligent fire or explosion might damage neighboring property. The standard liability policy does not cover liability for damage to property in the care, custody, or control of, or used or occupied by the insured. For additional premium, this exclusion may be eliminated, or this coverage may be available under the property policy.

Comprehensive General Liability (CGL)

This coverage may be contained in a separate policy or as part of a package. It will include both bodily injury and property damage liability for occurrences arising out of library activities, including ownership and occupancy of premises, operations, elevator liability, independent contractors, and products liability.

Suggested limits of liability will vary according to the geographic location, population concentration, library size, and business practice in the community. Due to changes in the legal climate, limits of liability should be periodically reviewed because limits considered reasonable in the past may no longer be sufficient. Minimum limits the library should protect itself with are $1 million combined single limit of liability for bodily injury and property damage, although some libraries may be prevented by statute from buying above certain limits.

It is advantageous to cover employees as additional insureds. The standard liability policy protects the library as well as individual directors, trustees, officers, and employees. Such coverage is important because, in most liability claims that are based on negligence, the individual employee who committed the negligent act may be equally liable with the employer. The employee normally does not have insurance under his or her personal insurance policies for business risks; therefore, he or she should be covered as an additional insured under the library policy.

Most general liability policies provide blanket contractual liability that will cover all contractual liability assumed by the library. Indemnity agreements in leases, sidewalk permits, easements, and elevator maintenance agreements will be automatically insured under a standard liability policy.

Product liability applies to the liability that might arise out of an injury caused by a product distributed to members of the public. This has relatively little application to a library's normal operation, but it could involve a risk where food is dispensed and consumed off the premises, resulting in injury. The premium charge for the coverage is nominal.

Dram shop, also known as liquor law legal liability, may be a necessity in certain instances. Some state statutes provide that anyone injured by an intoxicated person shall have a direct action against the one who served liquor to such person. The statutes may apply to hosts, such as one serving customers, employees, or benefactors. Host liquor liability coverage is generally available in these situations at a modest cost and should be considered by libraries serving liquor at meetings or receptions.

Coverage for property of others should be obtained in some cases. The property damage portion of the commercial general liability policy excludes liability for damage to property rented to, used by, or in the care, custody, or control of the insured. Fire legal liability coverage is intended to cover the catastrophe risk of liability for fire damage to a building that a library leases from another. The risk arises when an owner or its insurer (through subrogation) makes a claim against the library for an allegedly negligent fire.

Liability Insurance Rates

Liability premium is based principally on floor areas of library buildings. In most cases, insurance companies have some flexibility in rating and, where premium is substantial, actual loss experience of the library will be important.

Automobile Insurance

Auto Liability

Owned vehicles licensed for highway use are required by law in most, if not all states, to be insured for bodily injury and property damage liability. Minimum liability limits are set by the individual states. However, in most instances, the library should strongly consider purchasing coverage with limits at least as high as recommended above for commercial general liability; namely, $1 million combined single limit of liability for bodily injury and property damage.

The standard auto policy covers the library as well as anyone for whom the library is acting and any person driving library vehicles with the library's permission.

Physical Damage Insurance

Generally known as "comprehensive fire and theft and collision coverage," this coverage should be included in all policies. For ordinary vehicles, a $250 or even a $500 deductible for collision is standard. For expensive units such as a bookmobile, a higher deductible should be considered and may even be required by underwriters. A large library or institution with a fleet of vehicles may be justified in accepting a higher deductible or even self-insuring all physical damage, except for the catastrophe risk of fire or similar damage, if many vehicles are stored at a single location.

Non-owned Auto Liability

The library is subject to this additional risk. Under the legal doctrine of respondeat superior, an employer is responsible for the torts of his or her employee committed in the course of his or her duties. This means a staff member who is sent to the hardware store by the librarian—and drives his or her own car—will incur a liability on behalf of the library if an accident occurs. This applies even though the employee may be prohibited by library rules from driving a privately owned car. If the employee has auto liability insurance, the library will be covered under the employee's policy. However, the employee may have inadequate or no insurance. To protect itself against such a contingency, the library needs non-ownership coverage. This can include liability for all non-owned and hired cars. It is important library employees understand this coverage will be in excess of the employee's own personal automobile insurance.

If the library owns licensed vehicles, a comprehensive automobile liability and physical damage policy will cover all of the aforementioned exposures to risk. If it owns no vehicles, the auto non-ownership risk will usually be added by endorsement to the commercial general liability or the package policy.

Automobile Insurance Rates

The automobile liability and physical damage premium is based on the number of vehicles, kinds of vehicles, their garaging location, and use. In most cases, insurance companies have some flexibility in rating and, where premium is substantial, actual loss experience of the library will be important.

Umbrella (Excess) Liability

Umbrella liability coverage is written as a separate policy to apply as excess over the primary liability policies (commercial general liability and auto liability) in multiples of $5 million. For small public libraries, it may be possible for the municipality to list the library as an additional insured on its policy for a nominal premium. Limits greater than $5 million are not uncommon for public properties or where large groups may be assembled. Institutional risks are now purchasing even higher limits. A 2002 survey indicated average limit of liability even for small libraries (less than $200 million in revenue) was $43 million.

Usually, the umbrella policy will be broader than the underlying (or primary) general liability and auto liability policies. Claims that come under the umbrella, but that are not covered by the primary policies, are subject to a self-insured retention or deductible, which may vary from $10,000 to $25,000.

Workers' Compensation and Employer's Liability

Public bodies, including libraries, usually are subject to the Workers' Compensation Act and should be covered by workers' compensation insurance. The individual state law should be consulted in this regard. In any event, the insurance provides indemnity for the injured employee and protection for the library.

State statutes create a liability on the part of an employer for medical expenses and lost wages that an employee incurs as a result of a work-related injury or illness. The employer is responsible for payment of these expenses without regard to liability. In other words, workers' compensation is a no-fault coverage. Workers' compensation must be written as a separate policy. The coverage is mandatory in most states, and limits are statutory. Premium is based on payroll, and the policy is subject to audit at its expiration. The library may be justified in combining its coverage with another organization in certain situations.

Most workers' compensation policies include coverage for employer's liability, which should be purchased for situations in which lawsuits are brought against the library for employment-related suits not covered by the workers' compensation statutes. The standard policy will include an employer's liability limit of $100,000 per claim for employee injury that does not come within the Workers' Compensation Act.

In the states of North Dakota, Ohio, Washington, West Virginia, and Wyoming, and in Puerto Rico and the U.S. Virgin Islands, this insurance must be purchased from the state fund. In all other states, coverage is normally provided by private insurance companies. In those instances where the workers' compensation statute is not mandatory, the library should elect to come within the act if it can. This will guarantee benefits to employees injured on the job and will bar a common-law action for injuries.

Workers' Compensation Rates

Rates for workers' compensation are computed annually by occupational category on the basis of actual experience in each individual state. Libraries usually will have employees in two classes, and most states use the following coding to identify them:

- *Rating Code 8838*—Librarians or professional assistants, including clerical; and
- *Rating Code 9101*—All other employees (janitors, drivers, pages, and so on).

If the library has employees who do not fit into the categories defined above, the risk management consultant, agent, or broker can work with the library to determine the appropriate workers' compensation code.

In most cases, insurance companies have some flexibility in rating. Where premium is substantial, the library's actual loss experience will be important. The premium paid at the inception of the policy is considered a deposit premium and a final adjustment based on actual payroll is necessary at the expiration of the policy.

Directors' or Trustees' and Officers' Liability

Directors' or trustees' and officers' liability is another area of liability risk to which directors, trustees, and officers may be subject and which is not covered by the standard commercial general liability insurance policy. This is a risk similar to that intended to be covered by the directors' and officers' (D&O) policy written for business corporations. This type of policy undertakes to protect the directors and officers who might be sued by a shareholder on behalf of the corporation in a derivative action where the directors or officers have acted negligently or with poor business judgment and caused financial loss to the corporation. While the risks faced by a library's board may not be the same as a major for-profit corporation, people may be reluctant to accept appointments to boards without D&O coverage.

There are three forms of coverage that may be applicable, depending upon the nature of the library's legal status; that is, whether it is a nonprofit corporation, a part of a governmental body, or a public school district. The coverage described is not included or generally available in the standard general liability insurance policy. Relatively few insurance companies provide this special coverage.

Directors' or Officers' and Trustees' Policy

This form is most appropriate for the private, nonprofit corporation or organization. Coverage applies to liability for wrongful act, which is usually defined as any actual or alleged error or misstatement or misleading statement or act or omission or neglect or breach of duty by the directors, officers or trustees in the discharge of their duties, or any matter claimed against them solely by reason of their being directors, officers or trustees of the organization. This is generally construed to include violations of civil and constitutional rights, although the policy will apply only to directors, officers, and trustees, and will not defend employees who are not officers. There are numerous exclusions, including the personal injury liability risks that can be separately insured under the general liability policy; liability resulting from failure to purchase insurance; liability for fraudulent or dishonest acts; and liability for acts resulting in personal gain. When the corporation or public institution has adopted a bylaw provision for indemnifying officers and directors for liability for these acts, the policy also will provide insurance for the corporation or public institution.

Public Officials' Liability

This policy provides similar coverage and is appropriate for municipally owned and other public libraries. Coverage applies to liability for wrongful act, defined essentially the same as in the directors' or officers' and trustees' policy. Usually, it can be extended to include employees as insureds. This may be especially important to librarians and others in a supervisory capacity because it may present the only opportunity to provide coverage for these persons for civil and constitutional rights violations.

Board of Education, Public School Trustee, or Professional Liability

This coverage may be available for libraries that are part of a public school system. Usually, it may be extended to insure library employees.

Employment Practices Liability

Claims can be brought against a library for alleged violations of rights granted by several civil rights acts passed during the latter half of the twentieth century. Such claims can result from wrongful termination, discrimination and retaliation based on age, gender, race, or country of national origin. Such claims can be costly to defend, with expenses sometimes exceeding the cost of an award or a settlement. Employment practices coverage can be purchased as a stand-alone policy or endorsed onto a D&O policy.

Such policies usually contain a self-insured retention (SIR) clause to be paid by the insured in the event of loss. The policies are on a claims-made basis; that is, the policy covers claims made or first discovered during the term of the policy. This is in contrast with other liability policies that provide coverage if the accident or act complained of occurred during the policy term, even though the claim is made after the policy has expired.

CHAPTER 7
New Construction

New construction projects create new and unusual risks for the library. They also afford an opportunity to apply the concepts of risk management to the library's advantage.

Cooperation between the architect and the insurance agent, engineer, or consultant before the plans are finalized may help reduce fire hazards and make the premises safer. Delineating insurance requirements for the contractor will shift the risk of claims for accidents to the one whose activity is likely to cause those accidents.

The insurance considerations discussed in this chapter may apply to remodeling and maintenance contracts as well as to major construction projects.

Insurance Review of Architect's Plans

Architects should be aware of, and generally familiar with, building and safety code requirements. They should be required to work with the library's insurance agent, consultant, broker, or the insurance company's engineer, and to have the insurance company review and approve the plans.

Insurance Requirements for Architects

The architect should generally carry the same coverage as listed below for the contractor. Additionally, an architect should be required to provide evidence of professional or errors and omissions liability insurance, commonly called Architects E&O. This policy covers claims arising out of the negligent acts, errors, and omissions by the consultant, subconsultant, or anyone directly or indirectly employed by them. The coverage provided should not be less than $1 million on projects up to $5 million, or 20 percent of the value for projects costing more than $5 million.

Insurance Requirements for the Contractor

Before commencing construction, the contractor should be required to furnish certificates of insurance for:

- workers' compensation and employer's liability;
- commercial general liability, including contractual liability (insuring the indemnity clause described below) and completed operations (applying to accidents occurring as a result of defects in the structure after completion); and
- comprehensive auto liability.

Required policy limits should be at least equal to the limits purchased by the library on its own general and auto liability policy.

Owners' Protective Liability Insurance

A contingent liability coverage known as owners' protective liability is designed to protect the owner (the library) in the event there is a question as to whether an accident arose out of the construction project (and, therefore, is within the indemnity agreement). Some construction contracts will require the contractor to furnish an owners' protective policy in the name of the library. More appropriately, the library will purchase this coverage as a part of its commercial general liability policy, in which case the coverage will be described as independent contractor's coverage. The premium is based on the amount of the contract.

Hold Harmless

An indemnity (hold harmless) clause should be included in both the architect consulting and construction contracts. Because the owner (library) is usually liable for accidents on its premises when work is being performed, the indemnity clause is necessary to shift the responsibility for injuries back to the contractor who has charge of the work. Here are two samples:

- Architects hold harmless. The consultant agrees to defend, indemnify, and hold harmless the owner, its officers, agents, and employees from and against all losses and expenses (including costs and attorney's fees) resulting from any injury (including death) to any person, or damages to property of others arising out of the negligent acts, errors, or omissions of the consultant, its employees, or agents in performance of the work under this agreement.

- Contractor hold harmless. The contractor agrees to defend, indemnify, and hold harmless the owner, its officers, agents, and employees from and against all losses and expenses (including costs and attorney's fees) resulting from any injury (including death) to any person, or damages to property of others arising out of the negligent acts of the contractor, its employees, or agents in performance of the work under this agreement.

Surety (Performance) Bond

Public bodies generally are required by statute to secure a bond from the contractor guaranteeing performance of the contract, usually in the amount of the contract. This is protection against insolvency during the job, but also against the risk of liens that might be levied against the property for work or materials of subcontractors and suppliers whom the contractor has failed to pay.

Private libraries and institutions also are well-advised to consider the protection of such a bond.

Builders' Risk Insurance

Builders' risk insurance covers a building during the course of construction. Because both the builder and the library have an insurable interest in the project during construction, it is most economical to insure both interests in a single policy. The policy may be purchased by the library or the contractor, depending on the contract terms. Its essential features are as follows:

- the amount of coverage is usually the completed value of the building (a rate adjustment is allowed to compensate for the gradual increase in amount at risk);
- the builder's risk policies generally provide all risk coverage; and
- a deductible in an amount of $10,000 or higher may be required on the builders' risk policy. Usually, responsibility for the deductible will fall on the contractor who has the obligation to

protect the property. A specific agreement between the parties on this point is desirable. Generally, the contractor has more control over the construction site, and it is common to have the contractor either provide the builders' risk policy, or at a minimum, to be responsible for the deductible.

The builders' risk policy is intended to apply only during construction. Once the building is completed and ready for occupancy, the insurance company that provides the library's blanket real and personal property coverage should be notified so that coverage for the new building can be added to that policy. Where construction involves remodeling of, or adding to, an existing building, a builders' risk policy may not be necessary because the blanket building and contents form automatically includes additions and alterations. If the contract is for a substantial amount, it may be necessary to increase the amount of insurance under the blanket policy as the work progresses.

CHAPTER 8
Claims

Indemnity, a basic principle of insurance, states the insured should not profit from a covered loss. Insurance should restore the customer to approximately the same financial position that existed beforehand.

The insurance adjuster will be a key person in connection with losses and claims, although cooperation of the library staff also is essential. An important part of the insurance program is the assignment of responsibility for reporting losses and accidents that might result in claims. This includes instructions as to how and to whom reports are to be made.

In any major loss adjustment, it is a great advantage to the library to be able to demonstrate to the company loss adjuster that careful thought and study were given to the subject of values before the insurance was written. In every case where the library assumes or incurs responsibility for property of others, the library should endeavor to get replacement-cost values from the owners. The claims process, in essence, brings the risk management process full circle. Good and thorough risk identification and quantification will make the loss adjustment process considerably easier for everyone.

Prompt Reporting of Losses and Accidents

Most policies require the insurer be notified of losses and accidents quickly. This is necessary for proper claim-handling.

Major Property Losses

Timely and proper assessment of any claim depends on the availability of complete documentation. Listed below are documents commonly used by adjusters. If the library has all of them, the library and the adjuster will have little problem agreeing on the value of the library's lost or damaged property.

The steps taken immediately after a loss will affect the library's ability to return to normal operations as quickly as possible and determine the extent of the damage and the valuation of the property damaged or lost. Prompt action is critical to prevent damaged property from damaging undamaged property.

After notifying the claims adjuster of the loss, the following steps are necessary before the value of the loss can be determined:

- mobilize the emergency organization;
- protect library property from further damage;
- repair leaking pipes;
- restore fire protection;
- temporarily support collapsed or impaired structures;
- board up the premises and correct unsafe conditions, if they exist;
- isolate the damaged area wherever possible;
- separate damaged from undamaged property;
- restore power to critical areas, such as freezers;
- establish a loss account in the library's books, and charge all expenses incurred as a result of the loss to this account;
- retain all invoices, time sheets, and so on to ensure all costs are captured and attributed to the loss;
- retain any pieces of equipment or property that may be the cause of loss; and
- take photos prior to removal of any debris.

In order to document the value of library property, the library should have the following paperwork:

- invoices;
- purchase orders;
- repair quotations;
- time and material contracts with expenditures;
- labor time sheets with corresponding payroll journals;
- supply vouchers or requisitions;
- inventory quantities with pricing; and
- contracts for property of others, confirming insurable interest.

Finally, losses that include business interruption, loss of revenue, and extra expenses require the following additional information:

- additional expenses incurred to reduce the period of suspension of operations;
- reconstruction schedule;
- actual experience during indemnity period;
- actual experience immediately prior to the loss; and
- budgetary projections for time of loss and a period of time beyond date of loss.

Special Collections, Rare Books and Manuscripts, and Valuable Papers and Records

The library can minimize damage to rare materials by establishing a conservation service agreement before any loss occurs. Because most of repairable property damage in a fire is caused by water, immediate attention to water damage can drastically reduce the cost of restoring materials to their pre-disaster condition. A visual record of the condition of most valuable materials can help to determine the amount of conservation treatment covered by insurance claims.

For very old materials that may already have damage or considerable wear, it is difficult to determine the actual cost of conservation for a known incident without having first established the item's pre-disaster condition. If this precaution is not taken, disputes could result, impeding the chances for a prompt settlement. In the case of irreplaceable materials, the loss of a single item could be substantial. Establishing not only the value, but also the general condition on a yearly basis is key to settlement.

In any major loss adjustment, it is a great advantage to the library to be able to demonstrate to the loss adjuster that careful thought and study were given to the subject of values before the insurance was written. The total valuation summary should include a value for every significant category.

In every case where the library assumes or incurs responsibility for property of others, the library should endeavor to get replacement-cost values from the owners. In many instances, courts have hesitated to enforce a clause or waiver eliminating the responsibility of the library, but generally they have sustained an agreement as to value in the event of loss.

When an item is irreplaceable and there is no ready market for similar items, the value may be purely arbitrary and may depend on whether the proposed value is reasonable and how much premium the library is willing to pay for insurance. By insuring such items on a valued policy or agreed amount form, the insurance company accepts the stated value as the amount of loss if the item is stolen or destroyed.

Salvage

Damage to books resulting from a fire loss usually involves extensive water damage. Sophisticated salvage procedures have been developed that involve freeze-drying to prevent mold, and vacuum drying. However, whether salvage is practical will depend upon a number of circumstances.

For those books that are very valuable and irreplaceable, the library may be willing to accept the salvaged product, even though scars of the damage remain. For books that are replaceable, the decision will depend upon the replacement costs as these relate to salvage expense and condition after salvage. Salvage expense should include handling costs, reprocessing and filing, as well as contract costs for the salvage process.

Proof of Loss

Most property policies require proof of loss to be filed within a certain time period, although the insurer may extend this time limit. However, in any loss where there is a serious question of coverage, the library should comply with the provision or secure a written extension from the insurance company loss adjuster.

Workers' Compensation

Coverage requires an "Employer's First Report of Injury" to satisfy the Industrial Commission or other state body responsible for administering workers' compensation benefits.

Auto Accidents

Most states require auto accidents be reported on a standard accident form. The normal time limit is twenty-four hours from the time of the accident if bodily injury is involved, and ten days if only property damage occurs. The state form is usually acceptable to the insurance company.

Other Liability

All injuries to persons on library premises should be reported if it is reasonable to suspect a claim might be made for such injuries. Incident reports, however, should be made by the librarian and kept on file in the event a claim is later filed. It is desirable to discuss the reporting of such incidents with the insurance company, agent, or broker in order to develop guidelines to be followed. In the case of slips, trips, or falls, whether it is a claim or a nonreportable incident, the librarian should make an effort to investigate the incident. The report should indicate the nature of the incident, the alleged cause, and whether the librarian corroborates the cause. For example, if a patron states a fall was caused by water on a stairway, the librarian should immediately inspect the stairway to confirm the report. In some instances, it may be wise to take a photograph of the area to keep on file.

Cooperation with the Liability Insurance Company

The liability insurance company steps into the shoes of the library when a claim for injury is presented. This is true unless the library has a significant self-insured retention (SIR). An SIR is similar to a deductible in that the insured (the library) is responsible for the amount of the SIR. Generally, however, in the event of a deductible, the insurance company handles the claim and pays the net of the deductible. With a SIR, the insured library is responsible for claim handling with an obligation for reporting claims of certain types or above a certain amount.

When the claim has been submitted to the insurance company, the insurer has the legal right to full cooperation of the library's personnel in the defense of a claim or suit against the library. If there is a clear-cut case of liability, the insurance company will generally be anxious to settle with the claimant. However, settlement is the prerogative of the company, and the library should not make any commitments.

Because a claim may exceed the SIR, and the insurance company may ultimately handle all aspects of liability and workers' compensation claims, it is important all papers and communications that come to the library promptly be passed on to the insurance company. These may include bills, medical reports, claim letters, summons, and complaints constituting lawsuits.

Bibliography

Blackwell's Book Services. *U.S. Approval Coverage and Cost Study*. Accessed Feb. 22, 2005, www.blackwell.com/level4/coverageandcostindex.asp.

The Bowker Annual of Library and Book Trade Information. New York: R. R. Bowker, 1956—.

Breighner, Mary. "Colleges and University Can Take on Mother Nature . . . and Win." *URMIA Journal* (1997): 1–5.

Breighner, Mary, Barbara Carlson, and Gerald Naylis. "Modern Loss Control Protects Campus Value." *URMIA Journal* (1998): 31–37.

Breighner, Mary, Jeanne Drewes, and Gerry Alonso. "Understanding Property Insurance Values." *URMIA Journal* (2001): 43–51.

Drewes, Jeanne. *Library Insurance Bibliography*. 2005. Accessed Feb. 16, 2005, www.lib.msu.edu/drewes/insurance/insbiblio.htm.

————. *Useful Risk Management/Insurance Resources*. Apr. 16, 2004. Accessed Feb. 16, 2005, www.lib.msu.edu/drewes/insurance/inssources.htm.

————. Insurance Companies with Cultural Institutional Policies. Mar. 29, 2004. Accessed Feb. 16 2005, www.lib.msu.edu/drewes/insurance/inssources.htm.

————. General Collections Valuation. Jan. 12, 2005. Accessed Feb. 16, 2005, www.lib.msu.edu/drewes/insurance/inssources.htm.

Frisz, Michael, and Mary Breighner. "Maintain Effective Loss Control on Campus During Downsizing." *URMIA Journal* (1996): 4–11.

Goshay, Robert C. *Corporate Self-insurance and Risk Retention Plans, with General Reference to Fire, Liability, and Workmen's Compensation Exposures*. Homewood, Ill.: S. S. Huebner Foundation for Insurance Education, Univ. of Pennsylvania, 1964.

Insurance Institute of America. *Readings in Risk Management*, 1st ed. Malvern, Pa.: The Institute, 1980.

Insurance Service Center. ISO Products and Services. 2005. Accessed Feb. 22, 2005, www.iso.com/products.

Mehr, Robert Irwin. *Fundamentals of Insurance*, 2nd ed. The Irwin series in Financial Planning and Insurance. Homewood, Ill.: Irwin, 1986.

Myers, Gerald E., and American Library Association. *Insurance Manual for Libraries.* Chicago: ALA, 1977.

National Fire Protection Association. *NFPA 909, Code for the Protection of Cultural Resources.* Quincy, Mass.: National Fire Protection Association, 2001.

Reed, B. J., and John W. Swain. *Public Finance Administration.* Englewood Cliffs, N.J.: Prentice Hall, 1990.

Rejda, George E. *Principles of Risk Management and Insurance,* 4th ed. New York: HarperCollins, 1992.

Risk Management Resource Center, Risk Management Basics. 2005. Accessed Feb. 21, 2005, www.eriskcenter.org/erisk. htm?pid=108.

Trupin, Jerome, and Arthur L. Flitner. *Commercial Property Insurance and Risk Management,* 5th ed. Malvern, Pa.: American Institute For Chartered Property and Casualty Underwriters, 1998.

U.S. Department of Labor: Employee Benefits Security Administration. Compliance Assistance: ERISA of 1974. 2005. Accessed Feb. 16, 2005, www.dol.gov/ebsa/compliance_assistance.html.

U.S. Department of Labor: Occupational Safety and Health Administration. OSHA Home Page. Accessed Feb. 16, 2005, www.osha.gov.

U.S. Department of Labor: Occupational Safety and Health Administration. *Recordkeeping and Reporting Guidelines for Federal Agencies: Under the Williams-Steiger Occupational Safety and Health Act of 1970.* Washington, D.C.: Government Printing Office, 1986.

U.S. General Accounting Office. Terrorism Insurance, Implementation of the Terrorism Risk Insurance Act of 2002. Report to the Chairman, Committee on Financial Services, House of Representatives. April 2004. Accessed Feb. 6, 2005, www.gao. gov/new.items/d04307.pdf.

Vaughan, Emmett J. *Fundamentals of Risk and Insurance,* 3rd ed. New York: Wiley, 1982.

Williams, C. Arthur, and Richard M. Heins. *Risk Management and Insurance,* 5th ed. New York: McGraw-Hill, 1985.

YBP Library Services. New Titles. 2005. Accessed Feb. 21, 2005, www.ybp.com/ybp/DomIndex.html?title_reports.html&1.

APPENDIX A
Risk and Insurance Management Resources

General Information

Rupp's Insurance and Risk Management Glossary
This simply organized site allows the user to type a term or phrase into a risk management glossary search engine and receive contextual definitions.
http://insource.nils.com/gloss/gloss.asp

Florida Atlantic University Nonprofit Resource Center—Risk Management
Risk management is the attempt to minimize liabilities or the amount of loss of a nonprofit's assets. Insurance is usually the first thing most people think of when discussing risk management. The links on this Web site offer information about insurance options as well as the many other factors that may cause increased liability to a nonprofit. Topics run the gamut from protecting data integrity and addressing personnel problems and legal matters to covering the accountability of a nonprofit's board members. This site is intended to help identify risk and provide effective risk management techniques to nonprofits.
www.fau.edu/~rcnyhan/images/risk.html

RMRC Risk Management Resource Center
The Public Risk Management Association (PRIMA), the Nonprofit Risk Management Center (NORMAC), and the Public Entity Risk Institute (PERI) have created the Risk Management Resource Center to provide information that helps manage risk management programs more effectively. The center will ultimately include abstracts and the full text of PRIMA's and NORMAC's reference center collections as well as other databases, guides, and directories developed in the future.
www.eriskcenter.org

Public Entity Risk Institute (PERI)

Serving the risk management needs of local governments, small businesses, and small nonprofit entities, PERI's goal is to connect the library to the knowledge, resources, and information that will help the library address the risk management challenges.

www.riskinstitute.org

Insurance Information Institute (III)

110 William St.

New York, NY 10038

Tel. 1-800-331-9146

www.iii.org

Public Risk Management Association (PRIMA)

500 Montgomery St., Ste. 750

Arlington, VA 22314

Tel. (703) 528-7701

www.primacentral.org

Risk and Insurance Management Society (RIMS)

655 Third Ave.

New York, NY 10017

Tel. (212) 286-9292

www.rims.org

University Risk Management and Insurance Association (URMIA)

P.O. Box 1027

Bloomington, IN 47402

Tel. (872) 855-6683

Fax (872) 856-3149

www.urmia.org

Risk and Insurance Management Issues For Libraries

American Library Association

50 E. Huron St.

Chicago, IL 60611

Tel. 1-800-545-2433

www.ala.org

American Society of Appraisers
Tel. 1-800-ASA VALU (1-800-272-8258)
www.appraisers.org

Antiquarian Booksellers' Association of America (ABAA)
20 W. 44th St.
New York, NY 10035-6604
Tel. (212) 944-8293
www.abaa.org

The Appraisal Institute
550 W. Van Buren St., Ste. 1000
Chicago, IL 60607
Tel. (312) 335-4100
www.appraisalinstitute.com

Blackwell Book Services—U.S. Approval Coverage and Cost Study
www.blackwell.com

The Bowker Annual
www.bowker.com

Marshal and Swift/Boeckh (MS&B)
Tel. (213) 683-9000
www.marshallswift.com

National Association of Independent Fee Appraisers
Tel. (314) 781-6688
www.naifa.com

Loss Prevention Resources

National Fire Protection Association (NFPA)
The mission of the international nonprofit NFPA is to reduce the worldwide burden of fire and other hazards on the quality of life by providing and advocating scientifically based consensus codes and standards, research, training, and education.
1 Batterymarch Park
P.O. Box 9191
Quincy, MA 02269-9101
Tel. (617) 770-3000
Fax (617) 770-0700
www.nfpa.org

FM Global

FM Global is one of the world's largest commercial and industrial property insurance and risk management organizations specializing in property protection. The company provides information regarding property loss prevention resources.

1301 Atwood Ave.
P.O. Box 7500
Johnston, R.I. 02919
Tel. (401) 275-3000
Fax (401) 275-3029
www.fmglobal.com

Federal Emergency Management Agency (FEMA)

Federal Centre Plaza
500 C St. S.W.
Washington, DC 20472
Tel. 1-800-525-0321
www.fema.gov/about

APPENDIX B
Sample Risk
and Insurance
Management Policy

It is in the best interest of the (insert name) Library to make every reasonable effort to protect the health and safety of employees of the library and the public from any hazards incidental to the operation of the library and to protect its resources and assets, including the library's building(s) and its collections, against losses arising out of injuries, accidents, destruction and damages. Preservation of the library's assets and resources is a major responsibility of all employees. Managers are the custodians of the property that the library has entrusted to them, and they also are responsible for the safety of any persons who may directly or indirectly be affected by the library's operations. All persons with responsibility must, therefore, learn to manage those risks that could destroy or deplete their assets or that could harm any person. However, before these risks can be controlled, they must be recognized. To that end, the board shall establish risk management procedures to: identify risks; quantify and evaluate those risks; avoid them when possible without compromising the library's mission; take steps to reduce risks through loss prevention and control; and finance remaining risks by transferring them, when feasible, through appropriate agreements, the use budgeted of self insurance, or the purchase of commercial insurance.

By appropriate resolution, the Board of Trustees of the (insert name) Library on (insert date) has established the following policy in relation to its risk and insurance management program.

a. Responsibility for administering the risk and insurance management program shall rest with the librarian.

b. In accordance with the opening statement of this policy, it is the intention of this board to follow sound risk management practices. In that regard, the librarian is charged with the responsibility of identifying and quantifying the risks of loss to which the library is exposed; for developing, implementing and overseeing a formal loss prevention program; and for developing and implementing a comprehensive risk financing program incorporating self insurance and commercial insurance, including line of coverage, and in amounts reasonable to protect the library's assets and resources. For strategic planning purposes, the librarian should report to the board on the risk and insurance management program on a periodic basis, but not less than once each year. The report shall include recommendations, if any, for preserving and protecting the library's property, a list of insured and uninsured losses which have occurred during the past year, and an indication of possible risks of loss for which insurance is not currently available or has not been purchased, as well as information regarding the current insurance program, including a description of lines of coverage, limits of liability, deductibles and premium.

c.1. It is the policy of the board to insure catastrophic risks and to assume minor risks by budgeted self-insurance or by the use of deductibles, where appropriate. It is the desire of the board to limit aggregate annual self-insured losses to an acceptable percent of the annual budget. Toward that end, the board, treasurer, or other individual designated by the board will make a budget allocation each year to cover anticipated self-insured losses.

c.2. The librarian may designate an insurance consultant, agent, or broker to assist in the risk management process and to act as risk management consultant as deemed necessary by the librarian. The consultant, agent, or broker shall secure quotes from financially responsible insurance companies periodically as directed by the librarian. The consultant, agent, or broker compensation will be negotiated by the librarian directly with the consultant, agent, or broker. (Note: this responsibility may be subject to approval of the board or it may be delegated to the librarian or other person without needing the approval of the board.)

d.   The librarian shall promptly report all serious losses (as defined by the board) to the board.

APPENDIX C
Suggested Guidelines
in Museum Security

From the 1997 American Society of Industrial Security (ASIS) Standing Committee on Museum, Library, and Archive Security:

5.0 Fire Protection
5.1 Every museum shall be protected by a modern, electronic, early warning fire detection system which complies with NFPA standards and is listed as approved by Underwriters' Laboratories (UL) or a similarly acceptable testing laboratory.
5.2 All fire detection systems shall be annunciated within the facility both visually and audibly. Signals shall be clear, distinguishable from other signals and easily understood by all occupants of the building including people who are disabled.
5.3 Fire detection systems shall, in addition to local annunciation, be monitored at a second location that is monitored 24 hours a day, 7 days a week. These monitoring stations may be municipal police, fire or emergency dispatch centers or they may be commercial central monitoring stations. Commercial central monitoring stations should be UL-approved and periodically inspected and recertified by UL. These systems should comply with NFPA 71 and NFPA 72.
5.4 When a decision is made to use the services of an uncertified central station, the decision shall not be economic in nature and shall be with the advice of competent authority. An uncertified central station shall not be utilized without, as a minimum, an on-site inspection of its facilities by a person capable of assessing the ability of the uncertified central station to operate appropriately and with reasonable competence and security.
5.5 All museums should have fire-suppression systems. At a minimum there shall be portable fire extinguishers placed in strategic locations throughout the building in accordance with NFPA 10. Fire extinguishers shall be checked daily and inspected for proper maintenance monthly.
5.6 Automatic fire-suppression systems should be used. These systems may consist of water sprinkler systems, halogenated

extinguishing systems (after a careful evaluation of the environmental impact of such systems) or other automatic suppression systems. The most reliable system is the water sprinkler system; while a wet-pipe system is the best, a cross-zoned, dry-pipe, pre-action system can be used. It is best to install suppression systems throughout the museum but, at a minimum, sprinkler systems should be installed in all non-public areas of the buildings, especially offices, shops, and other work spaces, kitchens, storage rooms, loading docks, heating plants, wash and rest rooms, etc. Installation of these systems shall conform to one of the following applicable standards:

- NFPA-13 Standard for Installation of Sprinkler Systems
- NFPA-12 Carbon Dioxide Extinguishing Systems
- NFPA-12A Halon 1302 Fire Extinguishing Systems
- NFPA-12B Halon 1211 Fire Extinguishing Systems
- NFPA-17 Dry Chemical Extinguishing Systems
- NFPA-11A Medium and High Expansion Foam Systems

Author's Note: Regulations for gaseous protection systems have changed since 1997. Halon is no longer readily available and carbon dioxide poses a life-safety issue. The ASIS Museum, Library, and Cultural Properties Council is revising guidelines. See www. asisonline.org/councils/museum.htm for further updates.

See also American Library Association, Association of College and Research Libraries Rare Books and Manuscripts Section's Security Committee "Guidelines for the Security of Rare Books, Manuscripts, and Other Special Collections," www. ala.org/ala/acrl/acrlstandards/guidelinessecurity.htm

APPENDIX D
Property Loss Prevention Checklist

Make certain these points are part of the regular facility inspection:

Perimeter security:

Housekeeping:

Fences:

Exterior:
    Is fence in good repair?
    Yes _____ No _____
    Location of damage _____
    Date corrected _____

    Are combustible materials stacked away from building?
    Yes _____ No _____
    Location of damage _____
    Date corrected _____

Gates and Locks:
    Dumpsters secured and stored away from buildings?
    Yes _____ No _____
    Location_____
    Date corrected _____

    Normally secured areas locked?
    Yes _____ No _____
    Location of gate _____
    Date corrected _____

Security lights:
    Interior:
    All exterior lights working? _____
    Yes _____ No _____

Location of faulty light_____ _____

Date corrected _____

All debris removed by end of day? _____

Yes _____ No _____

Location of debris _____

Date corrected _____

Doors/windows/latches:

Sprinklers clear of obstructions (for example, by high storage):

Yes _____ No _____

Location of problem _____

Date corrected _____

All openings secured?

Yes _____ No _____

Location_____

Date corrected_____

Automatic Fire Protection:

Sprinkler control valves locked in:

Yes _____ No _____

Location of unlocked valve _____

Date/time corrected _____

Other points: _____

Immediately report to a supervisor any:

- signs of tampering with doors, windows, and security and protective devices
- false burglar or fire alarms
- unescorted visitors in nonpublic areas

APPENDIX E
Library Safety
Inspection Checklist

Date of inspection: _____

Areas inspected:

___ Auditorium/Facilities

___ Main floor

___ Second Floor

___ Outside areas

Persons conducting inspection:_____

    This inspection checklist is designed to aid the (name of library) in providing a safe environment for the employees and patrons of the library. Where deficiencies are noted, please mark the individual line item with an "X" and explain your observations in the space provided under the individual sections.

Emergency/Fire Protection

___ First-aid kits are readily accessible and stocked with adequate supplies.

___ Injury report packets are available with instructions/procedures.

___ Clear and unobstructed access to fire extinguishers.

___ Flammable/combustible materials stored away from ignition sources.

___ Exits are clearly marked and recognizable from interior of building.

___ Exit aisleways and doorways are kept unobstructed.

    Employees are trained in use of fire extinguishers.

___ Adequate number (four per floor) of employees have current first-aid cards.

___ Emergency phone numbers and names of first-aid persons at each floor.

Explain any deficiencies noted above:

_____

Building, Structures, and Overall Housekeeping

___ Floors are in good condition without tripping hazards or slivers.

___ Stairways and handrails are in good condition.

___ Ramps/loading areas are in good condition and free from tripping hazards.

___ Guardrails are installed and in good condition at elevated platforms.

___ Storage of materials in a manner to prevent falling or collapsing.

___ Restrooms are clean; shower and shower curtain are clean.

___ Waste disposal is timely in trash cans, restrooms, offices, outside areas, and so on.

___ Sidewalks, parking lot are free of large crack, tripping hazards.

___ Chairs, tables, desks, work surfaces are without slivers.

___ Elevator runs smoothly up/down (semi-annual).

Explain any deficiencies noted above:

_____

Environmental

___ Air quality.

___ Noise levels are excessive or cause complaints.

___ Temperatures too high or low, fluctuates, unable to control.

___ Vibration.

___ Illumination too bright, too dim, unable to adjust.

___ Ventilation is proper to control temperature, odors.

Explain any deficiencies noted above:

_____

Tools (Mainly Facilities)

___ Electrical tools have cords that are not frayed/cut, ground plugs missing.

___ Wooden-handled tools are free of splinters, broken shafts.

___ Metal tools are not bent, free of mushroomed faces, chisels sharp.

___ ll tools are stored in appropriate boxes, cabinets, not left lying around.

Explain any deficiencies noted above:

_____

Electrical

___ Switches/outlets are not cracked/broken, have secure covers.
___ Extension cords are free of frayed ends and cuts, kept out of walkways.
___ Circuit breaker panels are easily accessible with a three-foot clearance area.
___ All circuit breakers are clearly marked as to what they turn off and on.
___ All cords of any type are kept out of walkways to prevent tripping.

Explain any deficiencies noted above:

_____

Vehicles

___ Are vehicles kept clean and materials inside stored away from driver?
___ Is safety equipment in good order (wiper, turn signals, horn, and so on)?
___ Are tires, windshield, and brakes in good condition?

Explain any deficiencies noted above:

_____

Machines and Equipment

___ Copy machines and microfiche.
___ Any microwaves, refrigerators, and coffee pots.
___ Printers.
___ Computers.
___ Electrical powered desk equipment (adding machines, pencil sharpener).

Explain any deficiencies noted above:

_____

Chemicals, Fuels, and Lubricants

___ Are chemicals or fuel stored in cabinets?
___ Is protective equipment available as required by Material Safety Data Sheets (MSDS)?

___ Are warning signs and labels posted on cabinets where chemicals stored?

___ Are MSDS readily available for immediate use?

___ Is gasoline and diesel stored/marked in approved container?

Explain any deficiencies noted above:

_____

Miscellaneous

___ Ladders, extension and step type in good shape, not bent or broken.

___ Bulletin boards accessible, safety minutes posted, OSHA poster posted.

___ Carts to move books in good shape, free from rough edges, casters ok.

Explain any deficiencies noted above:

_____

Signatures of employees conducting inspection:

Date inspection reviewed by Safety Committee:

_____

Date inspection reviewed by Library Director:

_____

Action taken to correct deficiencies noted and by whom:

_____
_____
_____
_____
_____
_____
_____
_____
_____

APPENDIX F
Contingency Planning for Natural Disasters

The United States sustained $4.4 billion in insured catastrophe property losses during the first half of 1998 according to the Property Claims Services division of the Insurance Services Office. The natural disasters responsible for catastrophic losses—including severe windstorms, hurricanes, tornadoes, and earthquakes—can seem overwhelming. With advance warning, proper design and construction, and careful planning, much damage can be prevented.

The following checklists offer librarians questions to ask in order to identify, quantify, control and mitigate the risks of natural disasters.

Flood Planning

a. What are likely sources of flood waters, heavy rainfall, snow melt, or hurricane?
b. How will water enter buildings? Through windows and doors? Through plumbing systems? Gradual seepage?
c. What is the maximum water level expected?
d. How wide of an area will be affected by flooding?
e. Will the library become surrounded by water and inaccessible to emergency help?
f. Could flood water close down essential transportation routes?

Winter Hazards Planning

a. What equipment needs protection from freeze-ups?
b. Is heating equipment capable of maintaining building temperatures above forty degrees?
c. Are any facilities (such as book storage facilities) unoccupied? Does security check facilities on weekends and nights?
d. Are alternative fuel equipment and supplies maintained so they will be operational in emergency?
e. Are portable heaters and emergency equipment available?

f.   Are snow loads checked on building roofs? Is drainage adequate for melting snow?

g.   Will snow or ice prohibit access to buildings?

Windstorm Planning

a.   Are critical areas of the library identified?

b.   Are proper shutdown procedures for vital equipment known?

c.   Are back-up communications (cell phones, two-way radios) available, and phone numbers and contacts available?

d.   Is an off-site emergency center available outside of windstorm area?

e.   Are vital records protected or relocated?

f.   Do you maintain ongoing agreements with contractors for supplies and repair work?

g.   Do you inspect and repair roof covering prior to windstorm season?

h.   Do you provide shutters or plywood for window protection?

i.   Are storm surge or flooding potentials identified and emergency equipment available to remove water?

APPENDIX G
Sample Request for Proposal—Insurance Brokerage Services

Property and Casualty Lines of Coverage

Introduction and General Information

A.   The [insert library name] (hereinafter referred to as the Library) is seeking proposals from qualified firms to provide a full range of brokerage and risk management services including: marketing and placement of insurance coverage and consulting on coverage issues and self-insurance operations. One or more firms will be selected to fulfill these needs.

B.   The successful respondents will be required to enter into a five-year contract commencing [insert date]. The Library reserves the right to cancel the contract at the end of each annual period by giving at least 60 days prior written notice, or to cancel with cause at any time giving 60 days notice.

C.   To assist firms in preparing their proposals, general background information on the Library is provided in Section II of this request. For additional information, contact:

D.   All proposals must be received no later than xxxxxx at the office of:

xxxxxx

xxxxxx copies of each proposal shall be provided.

E.   The library reserves the right to waive formalities and reject any and all proposals.

Background Information

A.   The Library's property and casualty risk and insurance management program is administered by

Xxxxxx (insert name of person at the library responsible for the program)

B. The Library has xxxxxx locations, with total insurable values of $ xxxxxx. Library collections include:
Xxxxxx # of books, valued at $xxxxxx
Xxxxxx # of videocassettes, valued at $xxxxxx
Xxxxxx # of audiocassettes, valued at $xxxxxx
Xxxxxx # of microfilms, valued at $xxxxxx,
Etc . . .

C. The Library currently has xxxxxx full-time employees and an annual payroll of $ xxxxxx

D. The Library currently owns and operates a fleet of approximately xxxxxx vehicles

Performance Requirements

The successful brokers shall:

- Provide broker services for the Library in accordance with the requirements and provisions stated herein.
- Seek competitive programs and market lines of coverage on an unbiased basis and in the best interest of the Library.
- Conduct annual stewardship meetings and reviews summarizing activities and placements on behalf of the Library, including fees and commissions, and future plans.
- Prepare an annual market analysis and forecast by insurance line. This summary will include information on trends, market availability, pricing, and long-term market directions.
- Assist the Library in the design of policy forms and programs as needed.
- Verify the accuracy and adequacy of all binders, policies, policy endorsements, invoices, and other insurance-related documents, as needed.
- Issue certificates of insurance and answer coverage questions.
- Assist in the preparation of underwriting data, statements of values, specifications, and other data required by insurers.
- Assist the Library in preparation of proofs of loss or claims reports, and in obtaining loss settlements from insurers.
- Attend meetings as requested.
- Be fully qualified and competent with proper license, knowledge, experience, and personnel.

Evaluation and Award Process

A. The Library shall use its best judgment in conducting a comparative assessment of the proposal.

B. The Library shall select finalists that appear to have the ability to service the Library's needs.

About the Authors

Mary Breighner, CPCU, is vice president, global practice leader—education, public entities, and health care—for FM Global. Based in the company's Cincinnati, Ohio, office, Breighner oversees and guides the accounts and account servicing of more than three hundred colleges and universities, as well as hundreds of public schools, governmental entities, and hospitals worldwide. She is an active member of the University Risk Management and Insurance Association (URMIA), serving on various committees, as an officer and director and as past president. She received the Distinguished Risk Manager Award from the organization in 1992. In 2003, she was appointed to an affiliate member position on its board of directors. Breighner holds the Chartered Property and Casualty Underwriter (CPCU) designation. She has presented nationally and internationally on higher education and public entity risk management and insurance issues at numerous national and regional conferences, and has published numerous articles in *URMIA Journal*.

Bill Payton is a veteran of twenty-six years in the insurance industry, sixteen on the company side and ten on the insurance brokerage side. He has been director of risk and insurance management at the University of Missouri System since 1993. Bill was elected to two terms as president of URMIA, serving from 2003 to 2005. From 1993 to 2003 he served as chair of the risk management committee of the Midwestern Higher Education Compact, which manages a property insurance program for forty-seven Midwestern higher education institutions.

Jeanne M. Drewes is assistant director for access and preservation at Michigan State University Libraries. Previously she was head of the preservation department at Johns Hopkins University, Milton S. Eisenhower Library. She received her M.A.L.S. from the University of Missouri–Columbia and was a Mellon Intern for Preservation Administration at the University of Michigan. She is an active member of ALA, the American Institute for Conservation, and the Guild of Bookworkers, and has taught workshops and published on the topic of insurance and risk management, disaster planning, education, outreach, and other areas of preservation.

Index

Printed in the United States
64067LVS00002B/1-99